NUMBER TWENTY-EIGHT:

The Walter Prescott Webb Memorial Lectures

Essays on
The Changing Images
of the Southwest

[THE WALTER PRESCOTT WEBB MEMORIAL LECTURES]

Essays on
The Changing Images of the Southwest

Edited by
Richard Francaviglia and David Narrett
Introduction by David J. Weber

*BY RICHARD FRANCAVIGLIA,
OAKAH L. JONES, MARTA WEIGLE,
SYLVIA RODRÍGUEZ, AND
KARL DOERRY*

*Published for the University of Texas at Arlington by
Texas A&M University Press: College Station*

First edition

The paper used in this book meets the minimum requirements of the American National Standard for Permanence of Paper for Printed Library Materials, Z39.48-1984. Binding materials have been chosen for durability.

Library of Congress Cataloging-in-Publication Data

Essays on the changing images of the Southwest / edited by Richard Francaviglia and David Narrett; introduction by David J. Weber; by Richard Francaviglia . . . [et al.].

p. cm. — (Walter Prescott Webb memorial lectures; no. 28)

Includes bibliographical references.

ISBN 0-89096-620-6

1. Southwest, New—Description and travel. 2. Southwest, New—In literature. 3. Southwest, New, in art. I. Francaviglia, Richard V. II. Narrett, David E., 1951– . III. University of Texas at Arlington. IV. Series: Walter Prescott Webb memorial lectures; 28.

F787.E87 1994 94-18599
CIP

Contents

Preface

THE ESSAYS IN THIS VOLUME are an outcome of the Twenty-eighth Annual Walter Prescott Webb Memorial Lectures held at the University of Texas at Arlington (UTA). The theme of the 1993 lectures—Changing Images of the Southwest—has a broad appeal to scholars, students, and the interested public. By focusing on the Southwest, these essays also call attention to UTA's growing commitment to encourage historical scholarship in the region. These efforts have gained increased recognition through the creation in 1991 of the UTA Center for Greater Southwestern Studies and the History of Cartography. The center itself complements and works closely with the university library's Special Collections—a major archive of historical documents, maps, prints, and other materials—encompassing the vast region of the Greater Southwest.

The scholars who contributed to this volume represent a variety of historical, geographical, and cultural perspectives. David J. Weber, who introduces the volume, is Dedman Professor of History at Southern Methodist University in Dallas. Richard Francaviglia, associate professor of history at UTA and director of its Center for Greater Southwestern Studies and the History of Cartography, is a historical geographer. Oakah L. Jones, professor of history at Purdue University, is a specialist in the Spanish Borderlands. Marta Weigle is a University Regents Professor of Anthropology and former chair of American Studies at the University of New Mexico. Sylvia Rodríguez, associate professor of anthropology at the University of New Mexico, is the winner of the 1993 Walter Prescott Webb essay contest. Karl Doerry, professor of literature and director of International Studies at Northern Arizona University, is a film and literary critic

Together, these essays represent diverse disciplines approaching a singular challenge: to define and interpret the powerful visual and verbal images that have come to characterize the Southwest. As historians, we have ensured that one thing remains constant, namely, that the authors address the element of change over time in their interpretations. By so doing, we believe that this volume would have been welcomed by Walter Prescott Webb (1888-1963), the creative and brilliant Texas historian who did so much to inspire scholarship in the region of the Southwest.

RICHARD FRANCAVIGLIA
DAVID NARRETT

Essays on
The Changing Images
of the Southwest

DAVID J. WEBER

Introduction

In the early 1950s, British writer J. B. Priestley and his archaeologist wife, Jacquetta Hawkes, traveled to the United States to explore the Southwest. From Chicago they journeyed by train as far as Kansas City, then went separate ways. Hawkes continued west to New Mexico, Arizona, and Colorado to see America's oldest cultures; Priestley turned south to Dallas and Houston to experience America's newest cities.

The couple described their impressions in a single volume, *Journey Down a Rainbow* (1955). Not surprisingly, they found startling contrasts in the Southwest. Enchanted by Indians, Hispanics, and "refugees from the American Way of Life" (p. 9), Hawkes celebrated the desert Southwest as a place of enormous beauty with a sense of deep historical roots. Priestley, on the other hand, condemned Dallas and Houston as places without a past or, indeed, an inhabitable present. He deplored the homogenized urban culture as a "characterless mush of styles . . . imitation everything" and suggested that residents of the fast-paced urban Southwest needed to be "half-witted or half-drunk all the time to endure it" (p. 52).

In the urban Southwest, Priestley thought he saw the future, and he despised it. Hawkes had chosen to enter the traditional Southwest, and like many first-time visitors, she not only adored it but did not want it to change. Billboards and roadside businesses only scarred the magnificent landscape, she thought, and cars should be banished from the plazas of the quaint old Spanish towns.

The extremes of southwestern life—modern and traditional, urban and rural, tame and wild, ugly and beautiful, polluted and pure, mainstream and ethnic—remain with us today, as do the many shades between those stark opposites. Yet when we think about what constitutes the American Southwest, it is sublime landscape and premodern images that come to mind: dramatic canyon lands, brilliant blue skies, cacti and coyotes, adobe dwellings, and Indians living close to the land.

In our collective imagination, then, the Southwest represents a place of refuge from the modern, and we have gone to some lengths to maintain that illusion. The chic Santa Fe plaza is not only free of traffic in the tourist season, as Jacquetta Hawkes hoped it would be, but cleansed of businesses that might remind visitors of the workaday world. Pharmacies and hardware stores have yielded to purveyors of arts and crafts; boutiques have replaced grocery stores, banks, and the five-and-dime. Local residents shop elsewhere, abandoning the heart of Santa Fe to tourists. A similar process is well underway in and around the "old towns" of Albuquerque, San Diego, and Los Angeles; around the plaza in Taos (as Sylvia Rodríguez points out); and along the river walk in San Antonio. Entire towns—such as Madrid, Cerrillos, Sedona, Tombstone, and Jerome—seem to have more in common with theme parks or resorts than they do with living communities, yet these places have come to represent the "authentic" Southwest. Other communities, such as Los Angeles, Phoenix, or Dallas, may be situated in the Southwest but exist as worlds apart because they fail to exude stereotypical southwestern images.

How and why we have defined and redefined the Southwest and its distinctive images is the subject of the five essays in this intriguing little book. In the opening essay, "Elusive Land: Changing Geographic Images of the Southwest," geographer Richard Francaviglia deftly explains the Southwest as a political and cultural construction with elastic boundaries. When, for example, railroad builders penetrated the region in the nineteenth century, their definition of the Southwest followed the tracks. Initially, the Southwest included Missouri, Oklahoma, and central Texas; later, the Atchison, Topeka, and Santa Fe railroad shifted the region to New Mexico and Arizona. With the coming of the Santa Fe railroad, which Francaviglia identifies as "the most significant force in shaping the region's visual identity through image building," the Southwest shifted farther west, beyond Texas.

Those who do regard Texas as part of the Southwest often feel obliged to endow it with icons of the most scenic parts of the desert Southwest, no matter how inappropriate. The dust jacket of R. G. Vliet's Texas-centered novel *Solitudes* (1977—later published as *Soledad*) displays a man on horseback against a background of sand-colored mesas. "Why," Vliet asked his editor at Harcourt Brace Jovanovich, "does everyone in the East think Texas is in Arizona?" When the Dallas Cowboys played the Denver Broncos in the Super Bowl in 1978, the cover of *Time* represented the

Cowboys with the stately saguaro—a giant cactus that does not grow in Texas but in parts of southern Arizona and northern Mexico.

Richard Francaviglia also examines the Southwest as a place of shifting meanings, some of them contradictory. He describes how southwestern topography, regarded by one generation as hostile, came to be regarded as picturesque scenery. Americans who looked askance at the desert in the nineteenth century, for example, redefined it in the twentieth century as a "therapeutic landscape." Not all Americans share such a benign view of the desert, of course, and prior conditioning shapes our perceptions. As a tourist from Pittsburgh once told me, to him the desert looked like a "slag heap."

The idea that the Southwest, like beauty, exists in the eye of the beholder emerges with special force in the essay by historian Oakah L. Jones. In "The Spanish Written Word: Changing Images and Neglected Legacy of the Southwest," Jones takes us back to the sixteenth, seventeenth, eighteenth, and early nineteenth centuries. What is today the Anglo Americans' Southwest then represented the Hispanics' far North—the *septentrión* of New Spain and independent Mexico. Following a well-established convention among some Anglo-American scholars (dating back at least to anthropologist Ralph L. Beals in 1943), Jones refers to the borderlands on both sides of the present-day U.S.-Mexico boundary as the "Greater Southwest." In that large region, Jones reminds us, Spain's enduring legacy included the written word. Through recorded language in the form of diaries, journals, reports, letters, laws, charts, maps, censuses, and even rock carvings, Hispanics left us images not only of their own society but of the natural and native worlds as well. Without the written word, Jones makes clear, we would have few images of northern Mexico and the southwestern United States before the arrival of Anglo Americans.

With the coming of Anglo Americans, the meaning of the Southwest has continued to evolve, shaped not only by perspective and available information but also by the mindless gushing of hack journalists and hucksters. In the twentieth century, as anthropologist Marta Weigle shows us, southwestern iconography has been invented and reinvented at their hands. Drawing examples from the meanings attached to wooden objects—from the El Tovar Hotel at the Grand Canyon to kachinas, coyotes, and crosses—Weigle explains how image makers have both catered to the perceived tastes of Anglo tourists and, at the same time, shaped those tastes. Anglo Americans, for example, appropriate Hopi kachinas and Penitente santos, transforming them from wooden representations of the sacred, rooted in time and place, to decorative objects devoid of spirit. More recently, Anglos have commodified the image of the coyote—a folk-art fetish that derives less from the folk than from the demands of patrons and the handiwork of manufacturers, advertisers, and marketers. As one wood-carver, quoted by Weigle, notes, "I can make them lifelike, but folk art sells."

In Weigle's "woodworked" Southwest, premodern sells because it signifies a seemingly simple yesteryear. As Richard Francaviglia observes in his essay, "the strongest mythic component of the Southwest appears to relate to time, or rather our desire to stop it." When this involves the marketing of the anachronistic or the primitive as timeless objets d'art, no harm is done. When, on the other hand, the descendants of the earliest peoples in the region—Native Americans and Hispanos—become commodities to preserve in picturesque poverty, the consequences can be painful.

In a narrow case study with broad implications, "The Tourist Gaze, Gentrification, and the Commodification of Subjectivity in Taos," anthropologist Sylvia Rodríguez explores the impact of visitors and immigrants on the remarkable tourist mecca of Taos in northern New Mexico. In her subtle analysis, Rodríguez explains how artists, tourists, and immigrants found in Taos "an exotic, pristine world that assumed shape and meaning in contrast to the urban industrial world they tried to escape." In embracing the town, however, they also gentrified it. In admiring the "authenticity" of its Hispanic and Indian residents, the outsiders revived ethnic identities and strengthened ethnic boundaries.

Tourism, in short, transforms the very peoples and places that tourists hope will never change. Some of the most visited tourist sites become "museumized" as local people and outsiders conspire to present the image that they believe tourists come to see. And that image, as Karl Doerry explains in the final essay, is usually shaped by peoples outside the region to project their fantasies upon it. Doerry, a specialist in American literature, shows us those fantasies in fiction, film, and representational art. He demonstrates how we imagine the Southwest selectively, turning it into the antithesis of the modern city and its corrupting influences. The Southwest of the imagination, he tells us, celebrates "antimaterialism; a nonhierarchical, community-centered, tribal life-style; freedom from schedules, bureaucracies, and social obligations; and, above all, a sense of oneness with the world." Whether seen through the eyes of Mark Twain, Edward Abbey, or Tony Hillerman, the traditional Southwest represents the "dreamland of the world."

When their *Journey Down a Rainbow* led them to find "authenticity" in the traditional Southwest and artificiality in its urban centers, Jacquetta Hawkes and J. B. Priestley echoed the romantic values of tourists and writers before them and anticipated those who have followed them. Yet they missed an essential point that emerges clearly from the essays in this book. The romantic images of the traditional Southwest have been fabricated in the urban world of advertising and mass culture—what Priestley called "Admass." Moreover, it is urban areas that spawn most of the alienated travelers and immigrants who seek solitude in the Southwest; it is urban areas that usually generate the incomes that enable immigrants to build new lives in bucolic settings; and it is to urban areas that tourists often return, bringing the carvings, canvases, pottery, blankets, rugs, and jewelry that have come to symbolize the American Southwest.

While we may prefer the "sun, silence, and adobe" image of the Southwest popularized by Charles Fletcher Lummis, we cannot escape the fact that skyscrapers, smog, and suburban sprawl are also part of the region. Rural and urban not only sustain one another, they define one another.

Instead of continuing to see rural and urban as antithetical, however, perhaps we need to find new definitions—new images that combine the best of both worlds. Must there be a deadening sameness of urban life in the Southwest? Must southwestern urbanites leave their homes and travel to underdeveloped landscapes populated by exotic "others" in order to find sources of regeneration and renewal? Must retirees in search of new lives rebuild them in artificial communities where the quality of the golf courses exceeds the quality of the public schools in the urban areas they left behind? Must some of the region's oldest residents—Indians and Hispanos—live barren lives in picturesque rural settings? We must continue to concern ourselves with changing realities even as we contemplate the region's changing images.

RICHARD FRANCAVIGLIA

Elusive Land: Changing Geographic Images of the Southwest

The Southwest is a distinctive place to the American mind but a somewhat blurred place on American maps.

—D. W. Meinig, *Southwest*

There have been many geographic Wests, even if most of them have now changed their names so that we no longer recognize them as such.

—Cronon, Miles, and Gitlin, *Under an Open Sky*

THE GOAL OF THIS ESSAY seems deceptively simple: to identify the region called the Southwest and to describe those geographic features that make it distinctive. However, two words in the title—"elusive" and "changing"—should forewarn the reader that this is not going to be a simple geography lesson. It will be as much a study of cultural perceptions of what the Southwest is supposed to be as it is of what is actually there: like all regions that have become associated with certain popular images, the Southwest has become a state of mind as well as a place that can be identified, and mapped, by geographers.

Defining and identifying a region (which geographers tell us is an area having identifiable traits that set it off from the places around it) is a way of organizing and ordering our surroundings. Physical or tangible elements, such as topography and architecture, are among the more common elements used in identifying regions, but folklore and nonmaterial cultural elements, such as patterns of speech, are also extremely important in giving character to regions.[1] This essay will focus on tangible features that comprise a regional image, that is, what geographers call the cultural landscape. The Southwest can be defined in terms of its vegetation, land use, and settlement patterns—all of which are imprinted into the landscape of the region. This landscape is constantly, if subtly, changing. So, too, are images of it. Nevertheless, at any one time the landscape is a mosaic or tapestry that can be interpreted to reveal the dialogue between the physical environment and human culture, and between cultures—that is, between peoples claiming different heritages.

Regionalization is a convenient way of including, as well as excluding, both phenomena and people. Thus, a region is not a simple fact but is instead a complicated statement about what belongs—and what does not belong—somewhere. Thinking in regional terms encourages people to draw borders around places, thereby helping to divide the world, or portions of it, into more manageable parts. Whether one uses objective phenomena, such as rainfall (or lack thereof) and sunshine (especially the abundance thereof), or subjective factors, such as the feeling of southwesternness in a particular place, the process is much the same: decisions are made to include certain locations that belong within a region and exclude those that do not.

Regionalism is commonly expressed within both academic literature and popular culture. In the hands of academicians, this concept may seem scientific, but it is also always fraught with political overtones: whether helping scholars to describe the world, or political systems to govern it, regionalism conveys the power to order space and, in effect, to create place.

Regions, of course, are a fundamental manifestation of the way a culture or subculture both visualizes and verbalizes space. If, as the geographer Yi Fu Tuan has recently noted,[2] it is impossible to conceive of a place without language (and in fact language actually empowers us to create places), then the compound word *southwest* is very revealing. Two things immediately impress us about it: (1) relating to linguistic ownership, the derivation of *southwest* is northern European—actually English—instead of Spanish or Indian, and (2) the term can have several applications and uses: referencing both a *place* (geographic region) and a *direction* (composite compass bearing), it encourages ambivalence. Because the Southwest is a location (place to get to) as well as a direction one takes to get there, we subconsciously ask two questions when we hear the word *southwest*. The first pertains to direction, for we ask, southwest of what? The second relates to location, for we also ask whether the region is southern, western, or both (or neither) in character.[3]

As words go, then, the Southwest is ambiguous, but it is also evocative.

For most people today, it elicits immediate mental images of topography or geography (for example, scenery composed of red mesas and adobe houses). Such imagery is based on a series of elements, such as land-use patterns and architecture, that may appear outside of the region but seem to typify it when they occur there. Thus, when we visualize the region we interpret reality by ordering and constructing.

The term *southwest* conveys time as well as place, for the region is often described as having traditions associated with at least three major cultures that have interacted through time.[4] When describing its physical landscape features, the region's "primordial" or "ancient" status is often mentioned—as in the constant reference to time as well as space in the creation of its topographic features, such as the Grand Canyon, which, we are told, reveals geological history like so many pages in a textbook.

As a historical geographer, I shall emphasize the connections between time and place. This essay will analyze both historical and contemporary images of the region, showing where perceptual watersheds may be found in our vistas of the Southwest. Looked at this way, the Southwest emerges as a region that is constantly being defined, or redefined, by successive cultures that not only create mental constructs about it but in turn actually shape its landscape to conform to their perceptions and preconceptions.

This essay embraces all sources of southwestern imagery as important, for this region is inseparable from the totality of its literary, artistic, graphic, and cinematic images. Roadrunner cartoons, Disney nature specials, and feature films like *Thelma and Louise* can join the many journals, diaries, military records, and scientific reports in creating images of the region. Powerful images of the Southwest have been crafted by writers and artists, that is, through words (narrative) as well as pictures (still or moving graphics), reminding us that images are inseparable from language. Their words and pictures have made the Southwest part of our vocabulary and our collective psyche.

A SHIFTING REGION

Many people, scholars included, have defined (or attempted to define) the Southwest in more or less objective geographic terms. Readers seeking an understanding of the position of the region in the context of the continent's cultural geography are referred to Richard Nostrand's "A Changing Culture Region" in the encyclopedic *Borderlands Sourcebook*,[5] but are warned that anthropologists, geographers, historians, political scientists, and sociologists all offer different definitions. Some claim, for example, that Hispanic culture (and associated place names) are indicators of the region, while others may disagree by noting that Spanish culture characterizes several areas, including northern California and Louisiana, that are generally considered to lie outside the Southwest.

The issue of where the Southwest begins (or ends) is the subject of a seemingly insoluble academic debate that is expected to continue indefinitely—and remain a relatively unproductive investment of time and intellectual energy. Looked at critically, each of the maps that define the region says as much, or more, about the mapmaker as about what actually exists. Each map varies in design and motivation, and we may say that there are as many Southwests as there are people who define it.

Few of the maps offer the originality (and perhaps linguistic defensibility) of the Southwest "vernacular region" identified by geographer Wilbur Zelinsky (fig. 1).[6] This map is cumulative, or consensual, for it is based not on climate, topography, history, or culture but simply on the frequency with which people use the term *southwest* to refer to business enterprises and institutions. In other words, Zelinsky was not interested in defending any regional identity but simply in describing how people define it. We might say, then, that to Zelinsky, the Southwest is simply what people call it. His Southwest emerges as a large region that includes portions of Oklahoma, Texas, New Mexico, and Arizona. Based on popular nomenclatures, Zelinsky's map is significant for two reasons: (1) size: it defines a huge area, and (2) diversity: it recognizes the region as encompassing several smaller subregions.

By including portions of Oklahoma and even extreme western Arkansas, Zelinsky's map is disputed by those who envision the region as having tighter boundaries. Whereas Zelinsky offers a very inclusive and graphic definition, others, such as that of historian James Byrkit,[7] are exclusive and ultimately narrative. Although Byrkit references several maps of parameters and geometric divisions of the United States, he describes a much smaller region that comprises portions of Arizona, New Mexico, and, grudgingly, extreme west Texas. Byrkit defends the definition as where one can "feel" the southwesternness of the atmosphere, topography, and Native American (largely Puebloan) heritage. His definition is similar to that of D. W. Meinig, who, significantly, treated Texas as a distinct entity in the

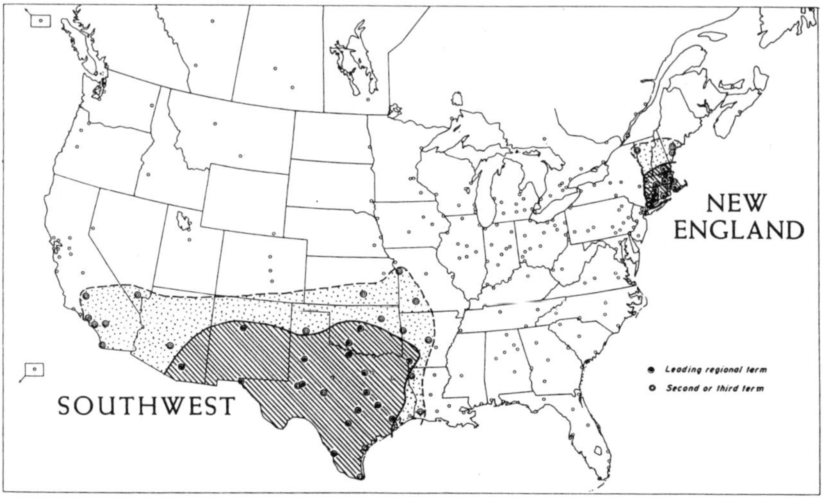

Fig. 1. Wilbur Zelinsky's map showing the Southwest reveals a large vernacular region where the name *southwest* is used frequently in naming companies and institutions. This map also shows another region, New England, which was influential in shaping images of the Southwest. (Reprinted, by permission, from *The Annals of the Association of American Geographers*, Blackwell Publishers.)

classic *Imperial Texas*.[8]

A word about the inclusion or exclusion of Texas in the Southwest is in order here. Whereas the public often includes at least the western three-fourths of Texas in its definition of the Southwest, many scholars exclude virtually all of it, preferring to label it "southern" when given the opportunity. Scholars often emphasize Texas's early, if not singular, push for independence from Mexico (1836) and its Confederate allegiance in the Civil War. The latter is significant since the diffusion of Texan and Confederate traits and traditions into the remainder of the region is visible in the cultural landscape and folklore. (There is even a portion of New Mexico called "Little Texas," and many Texas toponyms are found throughout the region, as well as the folkloric character "el Tejano.") During the Civil War, pro-Confederate sentiments and identity were strong throughout the region from Texas into New Mexico, through Tucson and much of southern Arizona to Los Angeles. Thus, the conundrum of whether Texas is western, southern, or southwestern appears to be based on the assumption that the state is monolithic (i.e., that its Texas political identity transcends any other index that might be used, such as cultural/ethnic identity or historical architecture) and that regions should not be composed of portions of states, especially a state that was once part of the South.

For practical purposes, much is to be gained by casting as broad a definition as possible of the region (hence the term *Greater Southwest*) and letting scholars debate where to draw boundaries around core areas. Broad definitions permit the inclusion of many smaller subregions of the Southwest (for example, northern New Mexico as the "Hispano Homeland,"[9] or the "Navajolands" of northern New Mexico and Arizona), which adds to the texture and complexity of the whole. The southwestern quadrant of North America is, above all, characterized by phenomenal physical and cultural diversity that regionalization tends to abstract or simplify. The more one tries to reduce this complexity, the smaller the Southwest becomes on one's mental map.

In recent years, some scholars have simply abandoned the term *southwest,* considering it an ethnocentric Anglo-American concept; after all, they say, it refers to the southwestern portion of the United States, and the Mexicans do not even use the term, referring to their part of the region as *el norte* (the north). Historically, this northern frontier area of Mexico has been characterized by immigration, intense political conflict, and much risk taking, as vividly described by cultural geographer Carl Sauer in his seminal essay "The Personality of Mexico."[10] These frontier traits, it should be remembered, are similar to those used to describe the character of pioneers in what is today the American Southwest. For our purposes, therefore, the southwestern portion of the entire North American continent along both sides of the border needs to be considered, for this region then emerges as a huge area where three major cultures—Native American, Hispanic, and Anglo American—have interacted, and have been in considerable conflict, for more than five hundred years. In the broadest of definitions, the Southwest is a vaguely defined frontier zone that mirrors cultural contacts and physical challenges, especially periodic or recurring drought; for our purposes we may consider the southwestern quadrant of the United States and the northern states of Mexico to comprise the Southwest in the broadest sense of the word.

IMAGING THE SOUTHWEST

Among the most revealing images of the region are those by mapmakers who put pen to paper and left a tangible record of inclusion and exclusion.

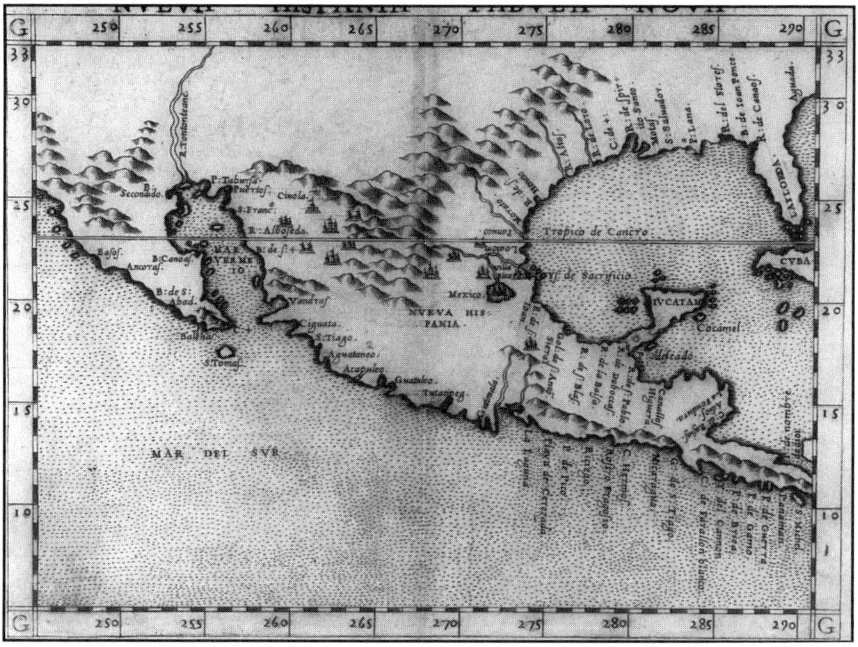

Fig. 2. Ruscelli's *Nueva Hispania Tabula Nova* was among the earliest of maps to depict the southwestern portion of North America as a region. First produced in 1564, the map was later revised and printed in 1599, as illustrated here. (Courtesy of Mrs. Jenkins Garrett, Fort Worth, Texas.)

Cartographically, the Southwest has a rich history. The first map of southwestern North America has been attributed to Ruscelli, who in 1564 (and later in 1599) depicted the region in words and pictures in the beautiful *Nueva Hispania Tabula Nova* (fig. 2). Cartographic historians have traced the imagery of the region's Spanish *entradas* as explorers penetrated the heart of the region within fifty years of Columbus's first voyage. Significantly, we might say the Southwest was discovered by Europeans more or less accidentally when Cabeza de Vaca began his seven-year trek back to Mexico after being shipwrecked on the Texas coast in the late 1520s.

By 1540–42, when Francisco Vásquez de Coronado trekked through the region in search of the Seven Cities of Cíbola and Gran Quivira, the Spanish had learned enough about the region to be disappointed in its material wealth and rather disillusioned by the peoples of the *gran chichimeca* and beyond. They also realized that the area's potential was dependent on how the sedentary native population could be appropriated and the wild, nomadic peoples "reduced." Coronado's expeditions mark a watershed in the perception of the region, for they gave a spatial dimension to the geography; they also summarized, and symbolized, half a century of Spanish dreams and failures in the New World. The region was vast, relatively poor in resources, and difficult to traverse.[11]

The seventeenth and eighteenth centuries (ca. 1600–1780) witnessed the impact of Spanish settlement. By 1609, the founding of New Mexico under the leadership of Juan de Oñate gave definition to the northern frontier. As the political geography of the Southwest developed under the Spanish, New Mexico later would be flanked by Texas on the east and the Primería Alta and California on the west, but it was to remain the northernmost settled area for more than a century. Thus, the Río Arriba represented the northern frontier's earliest outpost of authority, and the capital of New Mexico, Santa Fe, and its predecessor, San Gabriel, a strategic point along a major corridor into the interior of the north—the Río Bravo (Rio Grande) valley.

A careful study of Spanish cartography during the period would yield important information for those seeking to understand how the region took shape. After the coastlines were mapped in Portolan charts, the interior of this portion of North America slowly took shape as expeditions moved inland. The beautiful *Nuevo Mapa Geographico de la America Septentrional*, dated 1768, reveals the extent of Spanish claims and settlements in what would later become the Southwest. Maps of this type are instructive for what they do not show as well as for what they include. For more than two centuries, the region was mapped leaving large open spaces as unexplored *tierra incognita* where there was a lack of information about the peoples or geographic features. The amount of infilling corresponded not only to the amount of geographical information but also to the amount of pressure the Crown felt in defending its claims against other European powers, including France, England, and Russia.

The Spanish were masters of cartography, and their maps served several purposes: military, civil, religious, and economic. Their maps often marked the locations of native peoples and delineated communities. In any overview of Spanish cartography in the region, two processes become apparent:

1. Visualization. Early maps were often embellished with drawings depicting the topography, peoples, flora, and fauna of the region. Their images reveal a growing knowledge of, and appreciation for, both the size of the

region and the scarcity of knowledge about it. Parts of the Southwest remained *tierra incognita* until the end of the eighteenth century. Some cartographers succumbed to the irresistible temptation to fill in details where no information existed. This enhancement transcends naiveté and reminds us of the power of visualization as a basis for ownership: even fanciful maps stake a claim to reality, for putting a pen to paper implies a kind of appropriation if not outright ownership.

2. Politicization. Early maps of the region authenticated or validated Spanish claims, at least on paper. If taken at face value, one might assume that the area was under complete control, a condition that is not borne out by the historical record. In reality, Spain had perennial problems with its northern frontier, an area that was in periodic chaos as much as it was under control. Cartography provides one vehicle for bringing order to chaos, for one can use its persuasiveness to ascribe as well as depict order. Even if broadly drawn, maps of the early period usually interconnect places and depict political boundaries, that is, convey a sense of geopolitical order. These maps confirmed that the region was essentially an administrative outpost of a European realm. This northern part of New Spain came to be experienced as a series of isolated, nucleated settlements (whether native or Spanish in origin), punctuating a huge, seemingly uninhabitable landscape—at least uninhabitable by *gente de razón*. The region may have been perceived as being under the control of New Spain, but in fact Spaniards faced both physical and cultural barriers to their expansion.

Compared with the Europeans, the Native American populations had a very different relationship to the land and, consequently, a very different concept of the geography of the region. For the most part, native peoples lived two very different life-styles: (1) as sedentary agriculturalists (such as the Hopi), who had connections to centers of power to the south of today's border and were highly nucleated, and (2) as highly mobile hunters and raiders (such as the Apaches), who might remain seasonally in particular locations or return to them periodically, but had roamed the region for centuries. Native American peoples developed territorial or tribal divisions, but not of the kind imported by Europeans; even if the native peoples recognized their connections with others, it is unlikely that they ever thought of themselves as part of a geopolitical or natural "region." Thus, although Native American peoples are considered a crucial cultural element in most current definitions of the Southwest, there is no evidence that they ever conceived of themselves as such, at least not until the recent past. Regionalization implies a self-conscious geopolitical perception that arrived with Europeans.

Native Americans in the region certainly had cartographic traditions, but they would appear to be more pictographic, suggestive, and highly stylized compared to the more mathematically precise European/Spanish maps of the time.[12] Moreover, judging from the stylized, pictographic structures that native peoples left in many parts of the region, one may say that the landscape itself was part of their cartographic tradition—quite different from Europeans, who depicted places on paper as separate from reality.

The Spanish ultimately brought, some might say imposed, the concept of science to the Southwest, and they did it through maps and illustrations as well as the application of scientific technology. Their maps and drawings of the topography and environment often depict native and colonial settlements in detail and feature information about the flora, fauna, and peoples of *el norte*. This type of visualization helped shape perceptions of the countryside, and Spain's permissive attitude toward the internationalization of science in the late eighteenth century encouraged other European scientists to visit the region—and refine images of it.

Alexander Von Humboldt's map (fig. 3) is one of the watersheds in the perception of the region in that it exposed the physical anatomy of the southwestern portion of North America for the first time. This map is said to represent the dawn of the modern era of the scientific understanding of physical geography. It depicts the convoluted topography that reveals the Southwest to be straddling a backbone of two major mountain ranges and drained by a confusing network of rivers and intermittent streams. Subsequent scientific observation reaffirmed that the area was divided longitudinally into a series of ridges and valleys. This is not to say that Humboldt's map was correct, for it contains a number of significant errors.[13] On Humboldt's map, even rivers that today we know have more transverse courses seem to be constricted horizontally because of the cartographic inability to determine longitude effectively.

Despite certain errors, however, Humboldt's map reminds us of a basic fact of the region's geography, namely, that it is easier to traverse along north-south than east-west lines. This helps to explain the pattern of settlement in the Southwest for much of its history. Even under Spanish rule the area was compartmentalized along north-south axes, such as the Rio Grande in New Mexico and the Santa Cruz and San Pedro River valleys in Arizona. The topography also helps to explain the difficulty that rational people have in drawing lines around the region: there are no such physiographic borders in the landscape.

Fig. 3. Alexander Von Humboldt's *Map of New Spain*, published in London in 1810, featured the topography in great detail but still distorted the course of rivers such as the Río Bravo (Rio Grande). (Courtesy of the Special Collections Division, University of Texas at Arlington libraries.)

The transition from Spanish to Mexican rule (1810–21) witnessed the accelerating breakdown of Hispanic control as Anglo Americans began to infiltrate the region, especially into Texas and Santa Fe.[14] The migration to Texas was encouraged by a liberal immigration policy that began in the last years of Spanish rule and then continued for a brief period under Mexico. By the early 1840s, with Anglo supremacy in the north, the region was increasingly defined by a military presence: cartographic and scientific knowledge of the region greatly increased with the War Department surveys of the United States government. It was also defined cartographically by speculators who depicted parts of the region, especially Texas, as attractive to settlement. The maps encouraging colonists into Texas during the empresario period often contained phrases such as "well wooded" and "well watered" and depicted huge herds of horses and wild cattle. This is especially true of Arrowsmith's map of Texas in 1842, which actually describes portions of west Texas as "delightful," even though another map of Mexico in the same atlas depicts the identical area as "desert."[15]

The early nineteenth-century Anglo-American cartographic tradition of showing central and even west Texas as well watered and wooded defied the realities of the geography near the 100th meridian.[16] If, in the early 1840s, Anglo perceptions indicated Texas to be somewhat Edenic, this perception was being tempered by more sobering military reports that characterized the land between the Pecos River and the Rio Grande as marginal *llano*, or desert. The Mexican settlements of the Río Abajo and Río Arriba and scattered settlements in Arizona (Tucson and Tumacacori) were oases, or islands, in a land of rugged desert mountains, dry lake beds, and Indian tribes. Intrepid Anglo-American scouts and a few settlers had pushed into what would become the deep Southwest as early as the 1820s and 1830s, but, for the most part, much of the region west of Texas and south of Santa Fe would remain nearly blank on the mental maps of many Anglo Americans for another generation.

OPENING THE SOUTHWEST

Anglo-American understanding and recognition of the region that we call the Southwest is actually a relatively recent phenomenon. The term *southwest* appears to have been used first in the early nineteenth century (ca. 1803) to describe what some historians now call the "Old Southwest" the states of Alabama, Mississippi, Louisiana, and Tennessee. The Southwest became a region of empire and enterprise to politicians and entrepreneurs, especially those who were encouraging settlement in the Republic of Texas and, later, the building of railroads. In other words, the term *southwest* was linked to manifest destiny, for it was connected with the westward movement of Anglo Americans.

Among the watershed events that increased Anglo-American knowledge of the region, few could compare to the Mexican War (1846–48). Called the "Yanqui invasion" south of today's border, this episode in continental history witnessed thousands of American troops flooding into the region. In several major campaigns from Texas to California, American troops drove out the Mexican forces and continued their relentless push into the heart of Mexico. Their goal was southward and southwestward, thus, in effect, reversing more than three hundred years of episodic Hispanic expansion *from* the south and southwest.

Reconnaissance took place through a series of expeditions along and across what would later become the border between the United States and Mexico. After the war, numerous topographic expeditions set out to resolve the final position of the border and to determine locations for future railroad lines. The Bartlett and Emory surveys of the early to mid-1850s are among the most fascinating and informative, for their combination of scientific observations and utilitarian assessments foretold the application of Anglo pragmatism in developing the region. Symbolically, the final determination of the border occurred in 1853 with the Gadsden Purchase, which provided a route for the southern railroad line to the Pacific.

We may set the immediate postwar period, ca. 1849–57, as the time when nonmilitary Anglo information about the region increased exponentially. During that period the area was traversed by filibusters eyeing it for further expansion and settlement and by surveyors and engineers seeking the best route for what would become a web of regional railroads spreading into Mexico. The efforts of Bartlett and Emory, for example, were in part topographic—which is to say for the most part scientific and ultimately strategic. They contain numerous illustrations, some slightly romanticized, that exposed Anglo Americans to the scenery of the region (fig. 4). Other observers, including R. H. Kern, who traversed the region with Lt. James H. Simpson in 1849, left a vivid record of the cultural landscape of mountains, mesas, and pueblo villages (fig. 5). Travelers to the area shortly thereafter appear to have embellished material from the original reports, to the point that even original illustrations were enhanced in certain works:

Fig. 4. "Cultivated Fields and Villages of the Pimo Indians" appeared as a woodcut illustration in John Russell Bartlett's *Personal Narrative of Explorations and Incidents Connected with the United States and Mexican Boundary Commission (1854).* Illustrations of this kind helped Anglo Americans visualize the region and its exotic flora and peoples.

Fig. 5. "Pueblo of Zuñi," by R. H. Kern, depicted the type of Puebloan Indian village that became a regional stereotype. (From Lt. James H. Simpson's *Navaho Expedition: Journal of a Military Reconnaissance from Santa Fe, New Mexico, to the Navaho Country Made in 1849.*)

pueblos became larger, cliffs steeper, rock outcroppings more fantastic or fanciful.

Among the classics in this genre is Samuel Woodworth Cozzens's *The Marvellous Country*, which first appeared in 1875.[17] The geographic imagery conveyed in this book was pivotal in helping Anglo Americans fall under the region's spell, for the localities were often given surreal descriptions and their peoples stereotyped. Of particular interest to interpreters of southwestern imagery are comparisons of the original R. H. Kern illustrations as they appeared in Lieutenant Simpson's *Navaho Expedition* journal (1849) to embellished renditions of Simpson's work a quarter of a century later in *The Marvellous Country*.[18]

One of the most interesting perceptual aspects of the Anglo-American encounter with the region during the mid- to late nineteenth century, as amply illustrated in Cozzens's work, is the tendency to confuse the natural scenery with ancient man-made architectural forms. Cozzens describes the mountains of Arizona in the following terms:

> I never before saw anything so truly grand and wonderful! It scarcely seemed possible that the magnificent old castles, looking so proudly down upon us, with their towers and spires and battlements lighted up with such splendid effects by the morning sun, were but bleak and barren mass of rock, over which the foot of civilized man had never passed since its creation, or that the only notes breathed forth from the gigantic pipes of that mighty organ were those that woke in thunder-peals the solitude of the vast desert around us, responsive only to the touch of God's own hand upon its massive keyboard.[19]

Such poetic descriptions should be interpreted in the context of the westering experience and reveal the need to render the austere topography of the region in more familiar terms. Significantly, the topography is often described in terms of ancient cities, and these descriptions often have religious overtones: topographic features were named after temples, cathedrals, and castles. Cozzens even alludes to rock formations as resembling organ pipes, and the analogy did not stop with topography but extended to vegetation as, for example, when tall cactus plants are described as being "fluted with the regularity of a Corinthian column."[20] The vegetation of the Southwest was certainly evocative to Anglo Americans. Later in the nineteenth century, the Mormons gave the name "Joshua tree" to the distinctive *Yucca brevifolia* as they arrived in the southern portion of Deseret (Utah's Dixie), and travelers in the Sonoran Desert of southern Arizona named the distinctive fluted cereus cacti "organ pipes."

Fig. 6. "A City Not Made with Hands" graphically showed the kind of fantastic interpretations of scenery by travelers to the Southwest in the late nineteenth century. (From Samuel Cozzens, *The Marvellous Country* [1875].)

By portraying the landscape of the region as mystical, ancient, and fantastic, reports like Cozzens's often featured mirages and other ambiguous imagery such as "a city not made with hands" (fig. 6). Human and animal figures appearing in the sky and emanating from the landscape added an element of mystery to the area. These supernatural descriptions typify a Victorian Anglo-American way of viewing a new and unsettling region, but they also remind us that the Spanish were subject to similar imaginings. When viewed through shimmering heat waves or with a heated sense of expectation and anticipation, the landscape took on surreal qualities. Such imaginative descriptions were not duplicitous; they were instead to be expected of people whose traditions incorporated both scientific reasoning (objectification of the material world) and romanticism (appreciation of the mysterious).

Thus, the perceptions of this region were based in part on the search for truth as well as the ability to fabricate and embellish it. This mixture of fact and fiction became a part of the region's promotion by the railroads that pushed into it in the 1880s. Although the term *southwest* had been adopted by enterprising Anglo-American speculators who encouraged immigration into and development of Texas as early as the 1820s, the railroads put the term on the map by using it to describe the region in the late nineteenth century. The association of the term *southwest* with the railroads reminds us that eastern capital and power helped to define the area, which was southwest of the seats of power. These northeastern cities would ultimately develop the region's physical and scenic resources and define its character.

The railroads that entered the scene in the mid-nineteenth century were to transform permanently the region's geography—and perceptual images of it. In reality, our modern Southwest is a function of those railroads that were pushing southwestward from Saint Louis and Kansas City to the recently acquired Pacific ports of Los Angeles and San Diego in the 1860s and early 1870s. To these entrepreneurs, the Southwest meant Texas and the great Indian Territory (Oklahoma). But it also referred to their thrust southward and westward to the Pacific ports.

The Southwestern Railway Association was created in 1876 as a way of controlling the rapid development of duplicative railroad schemes in the region, and it is instructive to remember that John Murray Forbes has been called the "Vanderbilt of the Southwest."[21] As romantic as the term *southwest* may sound today, it was formerly used to describe the mundane but crucial landscape of Oklahoma, Missouri, and central Texas. Until its recent demise by incorporation into the Union Pacific, the Missouri-Kansas-Texas (or "Katy") slogan was "Serves the Southwest"—although it only served what some today call the Middle South. In truth, much of New Mexico and the austere land of Arizona that was parceled out of it—a vast area that is crucial to the region—did not have a nominally "southwestern" identity until the end of the nineteenth century, which is to say when the railroads finally realized their dream of reaching the Pacific.

Two railroad developments in particular—the Atchison, Topeka, and Santa Fe (AT & SF) and the Southern Pacific—helped to give the region its character. Both arrived about the same time, and we may say that the years 1879 and 1880 marked yet another watershed in southwestern history. Having beaten the Texas and Pacific Railway for control of the southern route from Texas to the Pacific Coast, the Southern Pacific constructed its "Sunset Route" (note the westering implications in that slogan) from New Orleans to Los Angeles, using its subsidiary affiliate, the Galveston, Harrisburg, and San Antonio, across the Lone Star State. In connecting San Antonio, El Paso, Tucson, Yuma, and Los Angeles, this line traversed the desert and mountainous zones from Texas to California. The railroad penetration into the region required that scientific data be translated into applied or practical guidance. Railroad survey reports were read widely, and their popularity confirmed the growing Anglo-American fascination with the area's economic potential as well as its aesthetic beauty.

The Atchison, Topeka, and Santa Fe lines also penetrated the Southwest, linking Chicago to the Pacific ports of Guaymas and Los Angeles through subsidiaries. Significantly, the AT & SF main line did not reach its namesake in New Mexico, whose capital city was reached by a branch line. In retrospect, the Santa Fe railroad improved on the eastern end of the earlier Santa Fe Trail and, significantly, provided a southwestward thrust toward coastal ports that had not been well connected to the rest of the region in earlier (Spanish) times; it rendered the manifest destiny of the Anglo Americans in steel.

The Santa Fe railway did more than embody the westward movement, because it became the most significant force in shaping the region's visual identity through image building. By the late 1880s, the railroad's promotional material had begun to emphasize a rather new commodity: the Southwest's scenery and peoples. In concert with the meal stops and crew/locomotive changes required in long-distance rail travel at the time, the railroad began marketing the image of the landscape and peoples encountered in the vicinity of northern New Mexico. Its timetables began to advertise stops, or sojourns, in what became labeled the "Land of Enchantment." Because the railroad's right-of-way ran directly past ancient pueblos and villages, it built them into its marketing: the landscape became merchandisable exotic scenery, and its peoples became cultural curiosities. Both became assets. Such promotion coincided with the rise of tourism in other parts of the western United States.

As has been documented elsewhere,[22] the Santa Fe railroad not only developed a visual image of the region but also sponsored architectural projects (such as railroad depots and hotel design) that perpetuated romanticized versions of the region's vernacular architecture. Furthermore, the Santa Fe railroad supported the arts through patronage and numerous art contests, encouraging talent to gravitate toward the Southwest in the early twentieth century. The railroad incorporated these images into its advertising from the early 1900s until about 1958. Memorable illustrations of mesas, mountains, and Indian villages helped cement the image of the "Land of Enchantment" (fig. 7), and the railroad's depiction of an Indian

Fig. 7. By the time this Santa Fe advertisement appeared in the 1950s, the railroad had marketed the region as the "Land of Enchantment" for more than sixty years. The use of spectacular topography and Puebloan Indian ruins had been a trademark of the railroad, and these features continue to be promoted by Amtrak's Southwest Limited into the 1990s. (Author's collection.)

boy named "Chico" helped reaffirm the region's ethnicity (fig. 8). One can argue whether such images of this colorful and romantic region were exploitative, but one thing is certain: like the early cartographers, image builders for the railroad helped create the impression that the Southwest was their territory and that their presence was endorsed by the native inhabitants.

Ephemera such as railroad timetables are significant conveyors of information and attitudes. In their use of text, maps, and other graphics, they reaffirm several important points, namely, (1) that cartography has many purposes, one of the most important being the validation of the sponsor's presence; (2) that portraying the landscape is always a selective process of inclusion, exclusion, and enhancement; and (3) that the coming of

Fig. 8. The colorful Southwest has ethnic overtones as Chico scribbles the Santa Fe railroad's slogan in the sand in this 1950 vintage advertisement. (Author's collection.)

the railroads introduced new concepts of time as well as place. The railroad brought the power of the clock and a regimentation of time along with other aspects of modern culture and technology. The latter ensured that views of the Southwest would be regulated or orchestrated much like theatrical performances. When dependable motorized transportation became available, the railroad used it to conduct "detours" into the enchanted landscapes of the region and in so doing further created the image of a scenic wonderland rich in ancient cultural traditions.

TIME AND PLACE IN THE SOUTHWEST

From the above discussion, we can see that "the Southwest" is a relatively new concept refined by westward-moving Anglo Americans, but that it is fraught with overtones of history and antiquity. Historical literature and popular culture emphasize the region's enduring traditions. Historians note that its long urban traditions can be traced back well before the founding of Santa Fe (ca. 1609), relying on archaeologists who date the Anasazi Pueblos at around A.D. 1000 and the region's agriculture at several thousand years before that. Significantly, what may be the oldest documentable archaeological site was recently (1991) excavated in New Mexico north of Fort Bliss/El Paso. Its age was reported to be a very respectably ancient 38,000 years. This, coupled with the fact that El Paso and its vicinity is considered by some to be the site of the nation's first Thanksgiving, helps focus popular attention on the Southwest and its history, which rivals, or even displaces, that of the eastern United States. Santa Fe is older than Plymouth, as the promotional literature reminds tourists.

In terms evoking its landscape imagery, the region is billed as the land time forgot. It is a land of ancient Indian villages, with timeworn topography deposited and eroded by millions of years of erosion that have left the rubble of petrified forests, volcanic cones, and meteoritic impact craters, looking—paradoxically—as if they had been formed yesterday. The promotional literature points to contrasts in attitudes about the Southwest: dinosaur digs and archaeological ruins are high points on the tourist agenda as entrepreneurs now market its antiquity as a sure draw for tourists, while at the same time enticing new or prospective residents into this part of the Sunbelt with claims of progress—high-tech jobs, leisure-oriented life-styles. The region's enduring environmental themes—temperature extremes (especially heat) and aridity—are packaged under the rubric of "sunshine," and have been since the hotels in Yuma advertised a free stay on any day that the sun did not shine.

This reminds us that the Southwest is, above all, a land of contradictions and dichotomies; it is both modern and ancient, commonly visited and mysterious, predictable and unpredictable. Its landscapes have been packaged; yet any particular advertising landscape may be a composite image that defies placement in a specific geographic location. With a very free hand, advertisers have mixed metaphors of time and space to produce images that abound in both anachronisms and geographic errors: cactus and other vegetation may be depicted where they would not normally grow; Indian dress may be switched; costumes or uniforms of Spanish padres and soldiers may be confused. These errors may be said to promote misunderstandings of the region at the same time they perpetuate stereotypical, and popularly accepted, images of it.

IMAGE BUILDING AS ART

Artists have affected popular perceptions of the Southwest by selecting natural and cultural features, such as mesas and adobe buildings. By rendering landscapes in certain kinds of compositions that emphasize the power of the sky and the shape of "tectonic" features, they have stylized the region's scenery. What has come to be called the southwestern style is closely tied to concepts of what belongs, and what does not belong, in the region. Viewed statistically, one finds certain elements or scenes overrepresented, thus stereotyping the landscape: saguaro cacti, adobe houses, and distinctive erosional topographic features, for example. Looked at geographically, many of the images of the area are abstractions of two locales: (1) the highland Southwest of Arizona and New Mexico from Santa Fe to the Four Corners and thence to the Grand Canyon; and (2) the Sonoran Desert in the area of Tucson to Yuma. These, not coincidentally, were the two parts of the region opened to early rail travel and were crossed by improved roads and highways in the 1920s and 1930s that closely paralleled the railroads.

Texas would seem to have been excluded from such "artistic" depictions of the Southwest, but in reality the west Texas landscapes of the Edwards Plateau helped foster the region's artistic image. It was Georgia O'Keeffe who began painting her sensuous southwestern landscapes in west Texas while she taught college at Canyon. Here, in the "Caprock Canyonlands" in and around Palo Duro Canyon,[23] O'Keeffe found a landscape of open skies and deeply eroded "badlands" that became the archetype for the muted but polychromatic landscapes of the Southwest. That landscape assemblage of dark, scattered plants (especially piñon) and richly colored soil and strata under intense skies (often punctuated by shearing cumulus clouds) became a stylized regional image by the 1920s.

The landscape of west Texas as a gateway to the Southwest is described by naturalist Joseph Wood Krutch, who in his popular *The Desert Year* wrote that "the change in the look of the land takes place suddenly and dramatically. . . . On top there is the plain of Texas, dryish but undramatic. Below, the red, eroded sandstone and the cactus declare that this is New Mexico a good many miles before the map makers have recognized the fact."[24]

To understand New Mexico in Texas, one has to travel the back roads of the Edwards Plateau. Even though this Caprock Canyonlands landscape is developed on a smaller scale than the canyon lands of New Mexico, it helps give Texas's Palo Duro Canyon the popular sobriquet sometimes attributed to the Coronado expedition: "Grand Canyon of the Red River." When shown color slides of Palo Duro Canyon and other Caprock Canyonlands images of west Texas and asked to identify the location, many audiences volunteer that the scenes were photographed in New Mexico or Arizona and have difficulty believing the west Texas locale. Those who use scenery as an index of the Southwest (i.e., those whose views are "topocentric") and who have not traveled in west Texas off the Interstate assume that Texas is part of the southern "Great Plains" and consequently not part of the Southwest. As regional indices go, topography is an attractive but deceptive indicator of the Southwest, but it is so ingrained that one can no longer separate scenery from the image. We can thank artists and photographers for this legacy.

A recent exhibit of art sponsored by the Santa Fe railway reminds one of all the ingredients—rose-red mesas, cobalt-blue skies, buff-colored adobes depicted in a variety of sensual, almost impressionistic styles—that are at the heart of the popular image of the region. The Santa Fe railway not only promoted a stereotypical image of the Southwest in paintings, it actually created a romanticized landscape to match the stereotypes, reminding us that art and commerce are interconnected in the region.

Architecturally, the fusion of "Spanish" and "Indian" styles has reaffirmed the region's underlying exotic but indigenous ethnicity to outsiders. Within two decades, the style became standardized and had reshaped the landscapes of Taos and Santa Fe into a collage of "soft," adobe-colored buildings set off by the angular openings of windows and doors and with Spanish colonial-style trim. Later institutionalized through building codes and zoning ordinances, the Santa Fe style has spread far outside of its original hearth to convey an important stereotypical image of the region (fig. 9).

Farther south, the Southern Pacific promoted its alternative to the

Fig. 9. The Santa Fe railroad's La Fonda Hotel offers a romanticized version of the region's vernacular architecture. The Santa Fe style has become institutionalized through city building codes. (Photo by author, 1979.)

highland Southwest: the "Espee" traversed the low passes and valleys of the Chihuahuan and Sonoran deserts, the latter, or low Sonoran, having the most delightful winters but almost unbearably hot summers. Most of the country along the Southern Pacific is part of the basin and range topography, a corrugated landscape of north-south–trending mountains and valleys. The landscape here is more subtly colored than that north of the Mogollon Rim: predominant colors are buffs and beiges in the valley bottoms and hazy blues of the mountains. In winter, the landscape is likely to be rather more lifeless in appearance than it is after summer rains.

This part of the region also has a symbol, the saguaro cactus (*Carnegiea gigantea*), which in reality is confined to a rather small portion of the Southwest (mostly below 2,500 feet in elevation at the western margin of the region). A few stands of these arborescent subtropical cacti are found in extreme southeastern California, but they are most common on rocky slopes in southwestern Arizona and northern Sonora. Nineteenth-century botanical illustrators were fascinated by this treelike cactus, which grows to a height of about fifty feet, and few southwestern scientific and railroad survey reports fail to mention, and illustrate, it. Easily stylized, the saguaro has become an icon for the entire region, although it does not grow in New Mexico or west Texas (fig. 10).

Iconographically speaking, the saguaro is easily transplanted. Although its home is the basin and range country in the southwestern portion of the region, we find it, quite improbably, in the stereotypical landscape images of Monument Valley. Two geographic features or indicators that are separated in reality by hundreds of miles—the stratified red sedimentary topography of the Colorado Plateau and the saguaro of the Sonoran Desert—have been integrated into the popular mind as generically "southwestern." These two elements are part of the fanciful southwestern country that came to illustrate the covers of dime novels and, in cartoon form, furnished the familiar backdrop for the antics of the "Roadrunner." Lest we think popular novels and cartoons are the only places one can find such botanical/geological fiction, we should recall the simulated saguaro cacti that were "planted" in Monument Valley for the filming of John Ford's *The Man Who Shot Liberty Valance* (1962). These helped to authenticate the location as the Southwest. If, as Lawrence Clayton recently noted, "several key cultural elements are perhaps more important than boundary lines, real or imagined," in defining the Southwest,[25] then landscape elements, as well as artifacts, are among the region's strongest symbols. That explains why the saguaro cactus has been used as a symbol by southwestern-themed restaurants from Alaska to Germany.

THERAPEUTIC LANDSCAPES OF THE SOUTHWEST

Students of the region's culture know that the Southwest has been infused with therapeutic or restorative powers by our culture during the twentieth century. Whereas many early European and American observers conveyed an impression of a godforsaken land of hostile savages, stinging creatures, and prickly plants, the region is now touted for the restorative qualities of climate and scenery. This, one might say, represents a classic

Fig. 10. The saguaro cactus is the region's premier icon of "southwesternness" and appears as a logo for the Saguaro Credit Union in Tucson, Arizona. (Photo by author, 1992.)

reversal in interpretation. Popular promotional literature cites the area's atmosphere, dry climate, scenery, and Native American (and perhaps even Hispanic) cultures as amenities, though history reminds us that as recently as a century ago quite the opposite was true. In the mid- to late nineteenth century, the place and its inhabitants were simply tolerated by most " pioneers" seeking wealth in the desert lands of the region. Some did find moments of the sublime, but these were rare. There is some evidence that the therapeutic or restorative qualities of the Southwest are linked to claims that one's physical health could be restored by exposure to its salubrious atmosphere, a claim that became more common around the turn of the century and especially after the First World War.

This topic, the Southwest as a place that can restore one's sensibilities and sensitivities, may have biblical roots: such renewal is inextricably tied to "finding oneself" in the desert landscape. The belief in the southwestern desert as a spiritual environment may be traced to the late nineteenth and early twentieth centuries. With improved transportation, notably railroads, one sees a new perception of the Southwest developing. It becomes an aesthetic, almost magical, realm of peculiar peoples and sights. The perception is largely visual, for the views and vistas are said to inspire.

By 1920, the literature was flooded with odes to the ancient peoples and to the primordial topography of the Southwest. As we have seen, writers of the period tended to confuse (or merge) cultural and physical aspects of the region. In 1921, John Gould Fletcher described "sharp-fretted, golden-roofed cathedrals" and "towers whose durable terraces were hammered from red sandstone." [26] To Anglo-American writers like Fletcher, the landscape became almost overpowering, as evidenced by his request for ultimate communion with the canyon lands:

> Should I by chance deserve some last reward from earth,—
> The rewards of earth are usually unwholesome;—
> One single thing I would ask for,
> Burn my body here . . . [where] . . .
> The winds would drift the ash
> Outward across the canyon;
> To the rose-purple rim of the desert
> Beyond the red-barred towers.[27]

More recently, film characters *Thelma and Louise* (1991) experienced a similar spiritual reunion with the Southwest. As they enter the region, these two female "buddy outlaws" give away the trappings of an earlier life (jewelry) and become more disheveled and sunburned (that is, seemingly more natural if not native) as they travel deeper into the Southwest. Being pushed first by circumstance and then by choice, Thelma and Louise become attuned to the austere, eroded landscapes of what they call the Grand

Canyon (actually first Monument Valley and later a canyon of the Colorado River). Seemingly as a result of what geographer Yi Fu Tuan called "topophilia," or a sudden encounter with the landscape,[28] Thelma describes the rugged canyon lands on two occasions by remarking, "My God, it's beautiful." For a moment, we may wish to compare this reaction with that of the Coronado party under Cardenas, who left no record of the beauty of the scene but merely recorded it as a singular obstacle. Thelma and Louise make the ultimate choice, artistically and spiritually speaking, as they take wing into the canyon (some optimists might hope that this leap would carry them across) in their symbolic Ford Thunderbird. This act of communion with the landscape assures that Thelma and Louise will achieve (cinematic) immortality. It also reaffirms the mythic, spiritual qualities of the region and its landscape.

CONCLUSION

The Southwest continues to be defined by powerful, evocative images of the landscape.[29] Those landscape images have in turn been shaped by Anglo-American appropriations of southwestern art, architecture, and topography. Byrkit states that "before we can understand the Southwest realistically we must first develop a sense of place based on a view that looks from the inside out instead of the New England Brahmins' and current trendy environmentalists' perspective of looking from the outside in."[30] In this sentiment, Byrkit invites emigrés and natives alike to salvage what is left of the region's uniqueness. One can expect any late twentieth-century search for the Southwest's true character to be inseparable from romanticized views of its heritage. Geopietism or geopiety is one of the strongest forces in defining the image of the region at present.

Having understood the many changing interpretations of the region, however, one must ask whether this geopietism reflects the Native American's spiritual relationship with the land or whether it is yet another form of appropriation. What Paul Horgan called the "Heroic Triad" of southwestern images—the mission/hacienda, the noble savage, and the cowboy/ranch[31]—remains very much a part of our perceptions today. To them we must add the image of the pristine Southwest environment as untouched by man. The preservationist/conservationist is emerging as one of the region's heroes, and his or her identity represents a continuing romanticism of the

Native American ethos.

All images of the Southwest are largely mythic in that they are perpetuated in the face of broader, overarching historic realities. Whether the home of nature, Native Americans, Spaniards or Mexicans, or cowboys (or miners, test pilots, Indian detectives, or conservationists), the region remains a place of high expectations and immense disappointments. To most people inside the area as well as outside it, the Southwest is a marginal land at the periphery of two giant cultural hearths. Lying at the northern fringe of Latin America and the southwestern fringe of Anglo-American society, the Southwest is always in a state of transition reflecting the shifting relationships between these broader national cultures.

Landscape or scenery has been abstracted, some might say manipulated, to reassure us of the uniqueness of the region. However, the contrast between vivid and mundane vistas has characterized the Southwest since the Spanish were first misled by the Pueblo and other Indians into expecting more, but finding less, than was there. For every beautiful view there are equally dull panoramas of scrub brush and unspectacular topography. For every historic adobe house there are a dozen mobile homes. But, of course, we see the landscape as we have been trained or conditioned to see it. Images of the Southwest today are liable to be very carefully orchestrated into scenic points, scenic turnouts, and gentrified historic districts.

Currently, two major countertrends can be witnessed in defining the geographic boundaries of the region. Through popular culture, one sees an expansion of the Southwest (or trappings of it) as xeric landscape plants and pseudo-Hispanic solidus Indian architectural styles spread beyond their geographic limits. Popular imagery in the form of idealized southwestern landscapes adorns T-shirts, pottery, shot glasses, and ceramic tiles. The image of the region has been expanded to include places peripheral to its core, as a coffee cup for Arlington, Texas, bearing the image of a saguaro cactus reminds us. As we have seen, in earlier times the Southwest was once farther east; perhaps it is spreading eastward again, or perhaps the entire southwestern quarter of the United States continues to fit in the popular mind as vaguely southwestern. Adorning homes and businesses with a southwestern motif helps this perceptual region spread beyond the range of its native plants and the locations of its most idealized (Native American Puebloan) cultures.

The second trend involves academic definitions of the region. There is some evidence that historians and historiographers, as well as anthropologists and archaeologists, are drawing tighter and tighter borders around the region, so that the Southwest is, in effect, shrinking. Looked at critically, many of these definitions seek to define "pure" cultures such as the Puebloan and Hispanic peoples of the Rio Arriba. In reality, of course, the region has been anything but isolated and its peoples anything but pure, at least not in the last five hundred years. The Southwest's marginality has invited exploitation and, only much more recently, protection.

The strongest mythic component of the Southwest appears to relate to time, or rather our desire to stop it, and thus preserve the traditions that make the region unique. This, of course, is impossible, but lies at the heart of every "Native" bumper sticker and those rather more to the point, including "Welcome to Arizona—Now Go Home." The Puebloan Indians may have repelled the Spanish in 1680, and the Apaches resisted the Spanish and later the Anglo Americans in southern Arizona during several crucial periods in history. Yet even the most enduring peoples of the mesa have assimilated many traits from other, later, arrivals.

It should not be surprising, therefore, that the Southwest emerges today as a haven of enduring landscapes and peoples, for such imagery helps an aggressive culture reclaim its innocence. In fact, as the region continues to change, we can certainly expect the conservation of pristine landscapes and the appreciation of indigenous cultures to become more popular, and more actively advocated. The Southwest's landscape images will be at the heart of the ideological discourse—and at the center of tourism—for they help us define an otherwise very ambiguous, and elusive, region.

NOTES

1. Barbara Allen and Thomas Schlereth, *Sense of Place: American Regional Cultures* (Lexington: University Press of Kentucky, 1991).

2. Yi Fu Tuan, "Language and the Making of Place: A Narrative-Descriptive Approach," *Annals of the Association of American Geographers* 81, no. 4 (Dec., 1991): 684–96.

3. Erna Fergusson, *Our Southwest* (New York: Alfred Knopf, 1940).

4. D. W. Meinig, *Southwest: Three Peoples in Geographical Change, 1600–1970* (New York: Oxford University Press,1971).

5. Richard L. Nostrand, "A Changing Culture Region," in *Borderlands Sourcebook*, ed. Ellwyn R. Stoddard, Richard L. Nostrand, and Jonathan West (Norman: University of Oklahoma Press, 1983), pp. 6–15.

6. Wilbur Zelinsky, "North America's Vernacular Regions," *Annals of the Association*

of American Geographers 70, no. 1 (March, 1980): 1–16.

7. James Byrkit, "The Southwest Defined," *Journal of the Southwest* 34, no. 3 (Autumn, 1992).

8. D. W. Meinig, *Imperial Texas: An Interpretive Essay in Cultural Geography* (Austin: University of Texas Press, 1969).

9. Richard L. Nostrand, *The Hispano Homeland* (Norman: University of Oklahoma Press, 1992).

10. Carl O. Sauer, "The Personality of Mexico," *Geographical Review* 31 (1941): 353–64.

11. David Weber, *The Spanish Frontier in North America* (New Haven: Yale University Press, 1992).

12. David Buisseret, "Meso-American Cartography" (paper presented at the *Entrada* symposium, the University of Texas at Arlington, February, 1992).

13. Robert Sidney Martin and James C. Martin, *Contours of Discovery: Printed Maps Delineating the Texas and Southwestern Chapters in the Cartographic History of North America, 1513–1930* (Austin: Texas State Historical Assoc., 1982), p. 43.

14. David Weber, *The Mexican Frontier: The American Southwest under Mexico* (Albuquerque: University of New Mexico Press, 1992).

15. John Arrowsmith, *The London Atlas of Universal Geography, Exhibiting the Physical and Political Divisions of the Various Countries of the World* (London: J. Arrowsmith, 1842).

16. Richard Francaviglia, "Cartography and Landscape: Early Nineteenth-Century Texas Maps" (paper presented at the Fifteenth International Conference on the History of Cartography, Chicago, Ill., June 23, 1993).

17. Samuel Woodworth Cozzens, *The Marvellous Country, or Three Years in Arizona and New Mexico, The Apaches' Home. Comprising Description of This Wonderful Country, Its Immense Mineral Wealth, Its Magnificent Mountain Scenery, The Ruins of Ancient Towns and Cities Found Therein, With a Complete History of the Apache Tribe, And a Description of the Author's Guide, Cochise, The Great Apache War Chief. The Whole Interspersed With Strange Events and Adventures* (London: S. Low, Marston, Low, and Searle, 1875).

18. Frank McNitt, ed., *Navaho Expedition: Journal of a Military Reconnaissance from Santa Fe, New Mexico, to the Navaho Country Made in 1849 by Lieutenant James H. Simpson* (Norman: University of Oklahoma Press, 1964). For an interpretation of nineteenth-century southwestern lithography see David Weber, *Richard Kern: Expeditionary Artist in the Southwest* (Albuquerque: University of New Mexico Press, 1985); and David Weber, "The Artist, The Lithographer, and the Desert Southwest," *Gateway Heritage* 5 (Winter, 1984–85): 32–41.

19. Cozzens, *The Marvellous Country*, p. 136.

20. Ibid., p. 53.

21. Charles Glaab, *Kansas City and the Railroads: Community Policy in the Growth of a Regional Metropolis* (Madison: State Historical Society of Wisconsin, 1962).

22. Sandra d'Emilio and Suzan Campbell, *Visions and Visionaries: The Art and Arts of the Santa Fe Railway* (Salt Lake City: Peregrine Smith Books, 1991).

23. Dan Flores, *Caprock Canyonlands: Journeys into the Heart of the Southern Plains* (Austin: University of Texas Press, 1990).

24. Joseph Wood Krutch, *The Desert Year* (New York: William Sloane and Assoc., 1951).

25. Lawrence R. Clayton, "The Southwest and Its Culture," *Journal of American Culture* 14, no. 2 (Summer, 1992): 7.

26. John Gould Fletcher, *Breakers and Granite* (New York: Macmillan Co., 1921), pp. 95, 99.

27. Ibid., pp. 97–98.

28. Yi Fu Tuan, *Topophilia: A Study of Environmental Perception, Attitudes, and Values* (Englewood Cliffs, N.J.: Prentice-Hall, 1974).

29. Kenneth W. Davis, "In Tribute to So Fine a Land: Popular Culture in the Southwest," *Journal of American Culture* 14, no. 2 (Summer, 1991): 9–12.

30. Byrkit, "The Southwest Defined," p. 386.

31. Ibid., pp. 352–53.

OAKAH L. JONES

The Spanish Written Word: Changing Images and Neglected Legacy of the Southwest

THROUGHOUT 1992 THERE HAVE BEEN many events commemorating the Columbian Quincentennial, or the five-hundredth anniversary of Cristóbal Colón's first voyage from Spain to America that forever altered the history of Europe and the Americas. While different points of view were voiced concerning "discovery" and the European impact upon Amerindian cultures, Colón's first voyage was unquestionably the central theme of the Quincentennial. As expressed by the Spanish government, this was an *encuentro de dos mundos*—the encounter or meeting of two worlds—the Old World of Europe and the New World of the Americas. Likewise, the Columbian voyage immediately brought two civilizations into contact and set in motion some five centuries of interrelationship, interaction, and change.[1] It should also be remembered that Colón himself made three subsequent voyages before his death in 1506. He not only explored and revealed Caribbean, Central American, and northern South American coastlines, but in his 1493–94 venture he colonized Española (today's Hispaniola) with more than fifteen hundred people, various animals, plants, and seeds, thereby establishing the first permanent European settlements in America.

This second voyage actually began the true "Columbian exchange" as described by many historians.[2] In approximately three hundred fifty years of Spanish and Portuguese presence in America, all sorts of products, people, customs, institutions, and diseases were exchanged between Europe and America. Spaniards introduced settlers—men, women, and children—who lived both in urban communities and in the countryside. Besides founding various towns, Spaniards applied place names to American cities, rivers, mountains, and other geographical places, many of which are still used today. They also introduced livestock—cattle, horses, oxen, sheep, goats, pigs, mules, and chickens—seeds, and plants—wheat, rice, bananas, garden vegetables, sugar cane, olive trees, oranges, lemons, apples, and grapevines—that would become the basis of agriculture in the Americas. The Spaniards carried back to Iberia maize, tomatoes, potatoes, sweet potatoes, cacao, indigo, avocados, chile peppers, peanuts, and tobacco. This exchange has influenced the diets and customs of both Amerindians and Europeans for generations.

In addition, Spaniards brought their language and traditions of family orientation as the basis of society, *dignidad* of persons, individualism, regionalism, and various institutions from the mother country. These included the Roman Catholic faith, bureaucratic administration, a mercantilistic economy emphasizing capitalistic profit, a close tie between church and state, and a special new social structure. Although not the same as in Spain itself, this structure emphasized *hidalgo* status and a complicated, dynamic social stratification based upon place of birth, *limpieza de sangre* (purity of blood), racial characteristics, wealth, and education. This new social structure incorporated Amerindians, blacks, and *castas* (mestizos or mixed-bloods) and was constantly evolving with each generation. Inadvertently, too, Spaniards introduced European diseases, such as smallpox, measles, typhus, diphtheria, whooping cough, and bubonic plague, as well as yellow fever and malaria. The latter two were carried from Africa by black slaves brought to America by the Portuguese, and later the English, for sale in Spanish slave markets ranging from Cartagena (in today's Colombia) to Vera Cruz (Mexico). Yet these same Spaniards carried back to Europe venereal diseases, especially syphilis, believed to have been originally introduced from Africa and Asia but carried back to Europe by the Spaniards' contacts with Amerindian women.[3]

Almost all of these examples of the Columbian exchange were present at one time or another in the region of the northern frontiers of New Spain,[4] including the area of the Greater Southwest. As Spaniards explored, conquered Amerindian civilizations, and settled north of today's Mexico City over the span of almost three centuries, the northern frontier changed. By the third quarter of the sixteenth century, it reached Nueva Vizcaya (today's Durango, Chihuahua, and parts of Coahuila, Sonora, and Sinaloa), as well as temporary settlements in Nuevo León and near the mouth of the Río Pánuco on the Gulf of Mexico. At the end of the sixteenth century, Juan de Oñate and colonists reached New Mexico and founded its first

Spanish town. During the seventeenth century, Spain's northern frontier expanded in places like El Paso del Norte (today's Ciudad Juárez), Sonora, Baja California, Sinaloa, Nuevo León, and other parts of Nueva Vizcaya and Coahuila. Finally, the eighteenth century brought a burst of Spanish expansion with the occupation and settlement of Texas, Alta California (today's California), and Nuevo Santander (today's Tamaulipas). This was accompanied by the settlement of Pimería Alta (the upper Pima region between the Altar and Gila rivers in northern Sonora, including today's southern Arizona) and the forty-year occupation of Louisiana, extending roughly northward along both banks of the Mississippi River as far as Saint Louis and beyond.

This expansion and the changing nature of the frontier not only brought Spaniards into the region now known as the Greater Southwest but also planted Spanish customs and traditions and promoted interaction with the numerous Amerindians on different frontiers. In addition, it contributed to the Spaniards' changing images of the Southwest. The Greater Southwest encompasses the huge area defined by the Adams-Onís Treaty of 1819, which also includes a substantial portion of northern Mexico and the southwestern portion of the entire continent of North America.[5] This region includes today's Texas; California; New Mexico; Arizona; portions of Nevada, Colorado, and Utah; the northern Mexican states; and Spanish exploration of the Pacific Coast extending northward from California to Alaska. In the late eighteenth century this exploration resulted in the establishment of temporary Spanish posts at Santa Cruz de Nootka on Vancouver Island and at Núñez Gaona (Neah Bay) on the northern tip of the Olympic Peninsula. The peninsula, which overlooked the Juan de Fuca Strait, was settled in the years 1790–95, the apogee of Spanish expansion in the Greater Southwest and along the Pacific Coast.[6]

It should be emphasized here, as Thomas H. Naylor and Charles W. Polzer have recently done and Rupert N. Richardson did in the mid-1930s, that the term *greater southwest* is synonymous with the region called northern New Spain in the colonial period.[7] This difference between viewpoints of modern citizens of the United States on the one hand and Spaniards and later Mexicans on the other must be kept in mind. Although people of the United States view their region as the Southwest, Spaniards and Mexicans historically and today view the region as northern New Spain and the Mexican North, respectively.

As noted earlier, Spain planted much of her culture, institutions, and

Fig. 1. The Spanish written word in the Southwest is found in many places, including this preserved notation at Inscription Rock in today's El Morro National Monument. It reads "Passed by here the Governor General Don Juan de Oñate from the discovery of the South Sea on April 16, 1605." (Author's collection.)

people into this region and left a legacy for the independent republic of Mexico after 1821. Furthermore, this legacy became a part of the historical experience of the United States and especially the Southwest after the 1848 Treaty of Guadalupe Hidalgo and the 1853 Gadsden Purchase from Mexico.

Though the Spanish language, Catholic religion, descendants, architecture, buildings, customs, livestock, plants, crops, and towns in the present southwestern United States—San Antonio, Santa Fe, Nacogdoches, Albuquerque, Los Angeles, Monterey, San Diego, and Santa Barbara—are indicative of this Spanish legacy,[8] one part of it has been overlooked and neglected: the Spanish written word. Broadly speaking, the Spanish written word refers to all documents written or composed by Spaniards—officials and private individuals—during the nearly three centuries of Spain's experience with the North of New Spain and the Southwest of the modern United States. This written word is evident in surviving documents that take many forms: maps, charts, town plans, census returns, journals, diaries, official reports, and letters (fig. 1). They include information of great value to historians and other disciplines on a variety of topics: administration and government, economic pursuits, the economy of regions, population characteristics, geographical features, flora and fauna, society and social structure, customs, military forces and defense, the Catholic Church (both secular and missionary activities), civil settlements, congregations of Amerindians, occupations and origins, problems of the frontier, and reforms made across the centuries.

Of special note is the constant Spanish preoccupation with Amerindian civilizations, often reflected in lengthy reports about the people we now call Native Americans. Spanish reports frequently gave detailed accounts of these cultures—for example, the Tarahumares, Conchos, Tepehuanes, Jumanos, Janos, Salineros, Coahuiltecans, Karankawas, Apaches, Pimas, Pueblos, Navajos, Hopis, Utes, Comanches, Nootkas, Taovayas, Yumas, *naciones del norte,* and California Amerindians—some of which have disappeared and others of which have survived to the present day. Often ignored or taken for granted by historians and deprecated by other scholars, these reports contained information about Amerindian locales, numbers, leaders, bands, weapons, fighting characteristics and practices, agriculture, women and children, diet, trade, hunting and fishing, languages, revolts, accommodations to the Spanish colonists, and assimilation into Spanish society. This information is of great value to the historian as well as the anthropologist, ethnohistorian, and sociologist, among others. Furthermore, these reports reflected changing images of Spaniards toward Amerindians across time. Views of these natives ranged from primitive, idolatrous, superstitious, lazy *indios bárbaros* (barbarians or savages) to intelligent, peaceful, valorous, loyal, and important segments of the population on various frontiers. These records are the first and often the only written sources we have concerning Amerindian cultures of the Spanish colonial period in northern New Spain, including the Greater Southwest.[9]

Spanish documents exist today in a wide variety and number of archival and library resources in Europe, as well as in America, especially in Spain, Mexico, and the United States. They are also found in London, Rome, and Guatemala. As one would expect, they are most extensive in Spain. About thirty-six million of particular documents exist in the Archivo General de Indias in Sevilla, but great quantities of them are also found in Simancas, Madrid, and Segovia. In Mexico the Archivo General de la Nación and Biblioteca Nacional de México, both in Mexico City, are major repositories of colonial documents, supplemented by regional collections in such cities as Durango, Chihuahua, Hidalgo del Parral, Saltillo, San Luis Potosí, and Guadalajara. In the United States important collections of documents and microfilm or photostats of Mexican and Spanish archives exist not only in the Southwest but at the Lilly Library in Bloomington, Indiana; the Edward E. Ayer collection of the Newberry Library in Chicago; the Bancroft Library at the University of California in Berkeley; the Henry Huntington Library in San Marino, California; the University of New Mexico Library at Albuquerque; the Nettie Lee Benson Library and Barker Library (Béxar Archives) at the University of Texas in Austin; the Special Collections (including the Janos and Juárez Archives) of the University of Texas at El Paso; the Laredo Archives at Saint Mary's University in San Antonio, Texas; and the extensive collections of the Documentary Relations of the Southwest project at the University of Arizona in Tucson. Other important collections can be found in Washington, D.C., Saint Louis, and Austin (the Nacogdoches Archives) and at the University of Texas in Arlington.

Illustrative of the changing images of northern Mexico and the southwestern United States during Spain's colonial years are the many maps, charts, and sketches composed by Spaniards and reflected on the maps that appeared in Spain and other European nations from the sixteenth through the nineteenth centuries. According to historian Harry Kelsey, the last two decades of the fifteenth century opened a period of stunning geographical expansion for Europe.[10] The quickening pace of exploration and discovery, begun earlier by the Portuguese along the African coastline and into the Azores, Cape Verde, and Madeira Islands of the Atlantic Ocean, led to the production of maps and charts of the known world. As the sixteenth-century explorations by intrepid navigators revealed unknown parts of the world, these geographical discoveries were depicted on maps compiled by cosmographers. In Spain this work was centered at Sevilla with the establishment of the Casa de Contratación in 1503. Juan de la Cosa was the first cosmographer there and the producer of a map of the Atlantic (including the Caribbean islands and coasts). The appointment in 1508 of Amerigo Vespucci as *piloto mayor* (principal pilot or navigator), along with the preparations of an official set of maps known as the *padrón real*, all established the Spanish practice of visually representing reports of navigators on maps and charts. Reflecting known geographical places, as well as inaccuracies and unknown areas, these forms of the Spanish written and pictorial record changed as knowledge improved. Navigators and mapmakers, therefore, informed not only Spaniards but the rest of the world about the "astonishing things that existed in this strange New World."[11]

These developments, of course, revealed maritime information including coastlines with unknown interiors until explorers, beginning in the 1540s, began to map, sketch, and describe the interior of the American continents. In the centuries that followed the expeditions of explorers such as Francisco Vázquez de Coronado, Hernando de Soto, Juan Rodríguez Cabrillo, and Bartolomé Ferrer, the geography of the North American continent was gradually revealed. It was reflected on maps and sketches—rudimentary at first, but improved in detail and accuracy by the latter half of the eighteenth century.

A few examples of the maps of northern New Spain (Mexico) and the southwestern United States in the colonial period clearly illustrate the changing nature of Spanish maps across the centuries. One of the earliest of these maps was that of Governor Antonio Oca y Sarmiento in 1667, providing the first known sketch map of Nueva Vizcaya (fig. 2). Accompanying his report containing suggestions to improve the defenses of his kingdom, the governor's map was a rudimentary rendition of the region north of Durango. It depicted the location of Amerindian villages and Spanish communities, the Sierra Madre Occidental, rivers, sites for the governor's proposed watchtowers, and regions in which Amerindian *amigos* dwelled, as well as those areas infested with Amerindian *enemigos*.[12]

Although this map does not depict the present southwestern portion of today's United States, it is an early expression of the Greater Southwest in the latter half of the seventeenth century. By the early eighteenth century the explorations of Jesuit missionary Eusebio Francisco Kino in Pimería Alta were portrayed on his maps, drawn before his death in 1711. These examples of the Spanish written word show not only the places he visited, including his observation that *California no es una isla* (California, meaning Baja California, is not an island), but also geographical features of the land and names of groups or tribes living there, which were noted in large colored letters across his maps. Rejecting earlier geographical misconceptions, Kino's maps were "progressive," even more inclusive and more accurate than previous ones, reflecting his growing knowledge of that portion of the Greater Southwest.[13]

More detailed, extensive, and accurate maps prepared by Spanish officials in the latter half of the eighteenth century also illustrated the changing nature of images concerning the region. Improving on those maps of

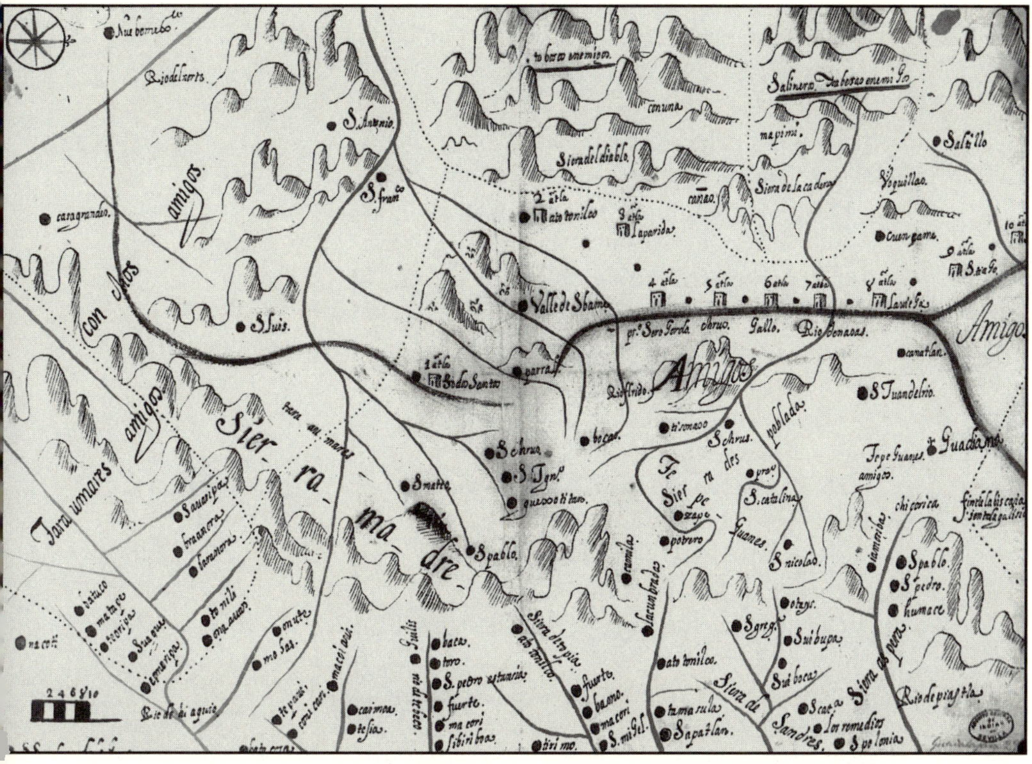

Fig. 2. This map of Nueva Vizcaya, 1667, contains suggestions on improving the Crown's defenses and depicts Amerindian and Spanish communities as well as aspects of the region's physical geography. (From the Archivo General de Indias, Mapas y Planos, México, 615.)

the engineer Francisco Alvarez Barreiro, who had accompanied Brigadier Pedro de Rivera on his inspection of the northern frontier of New Spain from 1724 to 1728,[14] engineer Nicolás de Lafora drew a detailed map of northern New Spain. This map, which included Texas, New Mexico, and adjacent interior regions, was derived from his participation in the inspection of the Marqués de Rubí from 1766 to 1768.[15] Lieutenant José Urrutia, who also accompanied Rubí and Lafora, rendered in color precise plans and elevation views of existing presidios in today's Mexico and the southwestern United States, twenty-one of which are preserved in the British Museum in London.[16] Bernardo Miera y Pacheco, soldier, cartographer, and *santero* (carver of holy images) of New Mexico, who accompanied Fathers Francisco Atanasio Domínguez and Silvestre Vélez de Escalante to Utah and much of the Southwest, composed a detailed map of New Mexico and its environs in 1779. Not only did it depict geographical features, but its legend contained important historical information describing settlements, Pueblo Indian villages, the region of El Paso del Norte, an attack of Comanches, and Apache enemies.[17]

Finally, for examples of changing Spanish images of the Pacific Coast, Alta and Baja California, the Northwest, and Alaska, there are maps, charts, and sketches drawn by Spanish navigators and artists from 1774 to 1795. Francisco de la Bodega y Quadra, Esteban Josef Martínez, Salvador Fidalgo, José Mariano Moziño, and Tomás de Suría provided not only maps and charts depicting geographical knowledge of that time but sketches and drawings showing elevations of the land and the Amerindians of Nootka Sound and elsewhere.[18]

Thus maps, charts, and *planos* (plans) of Spaniards over the course of nearly three centuries expressed the changing images of the Greater Southwest. As examples of the Spanish written word, they are valuable as descriptions of geographical information and for the historical material they contain. Together with their informative legends and the reports they accompanied, they are, as Father Ernest J. Burrus described Father Kino's maps, "a visual aid to understand a geographical reality."[19]

Other examples of the Spanish written word include reports, diaries, journals, letters, and especially census returns written by both secular and ecclesiastical officials, as well as those of private individuals. These documents concerned matters ranging from the empire to local municipalities. They included reports of viceroys, governors, bishops, clergymen, and royal inspectors, such as those of Joseph Francisco Marín, Pedro de Rivera, the Marqués de Rubí, and Bishop Pedro Tamarón y Romeral.[20]

Of special note are the census returns compiled from 1776 to 1821 following King Carlos III's order of 1776. Although not accomplished every year and varying in their content, *padrones* (censuses) were completed by both civil and religious officials for Spanish and Amerindian communities during this period. They were of two types: one was a statistical table reflecting numbers of people; origins; ages; families; classes; occupations; subheadings of men, women, and children; and animals and properties possessed by individuals. The other was a listing of families (both men and women, single and married); ages; occupations; marital status; children; servants; relatives; and others attached to each household, including Amerindians. Together these two types of censuses provide much information on a wide variety of topics in addition to demographical data. Studied carefully, they also reveal changes in families and the population of Spanish civil settlements and Amerindian villages.

Although it would be tedious and inappropriate to examine in this study every census, two examples clearly illustrate their importance to historians and scholars in other disciplines. First, the census of Texas's governor, the Barón de Ripperdá, of November 6, 1777, indicated that 3,103 Spaniards, mixed-bloods (*castas*), and peacefully settled Amerindians lived in the province of Texas. This total included 1,141 men, 902 women, 1,040 children, and 20 slaves. Nearly 56 percent of the men were married, and 114 of them were widowers.[21] Later censuses and reports of governors, such as that of Manuel María de Salcedo y Quiroga in 1809, showed a fairly stable population for the province of Texas, reaching 3,980 people in 1804 and 4,155 (3,122 settlers and 1,033 soldiers) five years later in six jurisdictions.[22] A detailed list of troops and settlers at La Bahía in 1780 provided not only numbers of people but lists of individuals and families by name in a seven-page document. From it one can obtain information about persons, classes, ages, origins, occupations, marital status, number of children, servants living with families, armament, and material possessions, as well as animals possessed by each head of a household.[23] A similar list of 308 families at San Fernando de Béxar (today's San Antonio) in 1792 provided extensive and important information on the people of that community. In this census and others, for example, Texas residents were principally engaged in small farming; worked as day laborers, merchants, and traders, such as "barbers and bleeders"; and were tailors, shoemakers, and blacksmiths, as well as masons, carpenters, hatmakers, mule drivers (*arrieros*), and servants.[24]

A second example of information derived from Spanish censuses can be cited for New Mexico. Although there were earlier ones, those of 1790 and 1810 were most detailed and useful. The *padrones* that made up parts of the overall census of 1790 pertained to Spanish civil settlements, such as Santa Fe, Albuquerque, El Paso del Norte, Santa Cruz de la Cañada, and the northern jurisdictions. They also contained information from Pueblo Indian villages, such as Santo Domingo, Cochití, Acoma, San Juan, Santa Clara, and San Ildefonso. Altogether these censuses reflected a total population of 30,953 in 1790, including 5,244 at El Paso del Norte, 3,733 in Santa Fe, 5,929 in Albuquerque, and 8,895 at La Cañada and its environs.[25] Two-thirds of the population were classified as *españoles* (Spaniards, including those born in America and persons having a Spanish life-style) and *castas* (persons of mixed races). It is also evident that some acculturated Amerindians lived in the Spanish communities and that some native men were married to Spanish women, while some Spanish families lived in or near Pueblo Indian villages in violation of royal laws to keep the two cultures separate. Of special value in this census are the family listings by jurisdiction with both men and women as heads of families and property owners. Carefully studied for the information they contain, these examples of the Spanish written word reveal names of persons, ages, racial status, *castas*, occupations, relatives, origins, servants, slaves, and size of families.[26]

Perhaps a few examples from the general census of the jurisdiction of San Felipe de Albuquerque in the province of New Mexico, October 22, 1790, will illustrate the nature of information conveyed by the Spanish written word. Of the 909 heads of families listed, they included:[27]

1. The Señor *alcalde* (mayor) Don Manuel Arteaga, Spaniard, fifty-three years old, native of the city of México, widower, resident in the town of San Agustín de Ysleta; one son, twenty-three years old (family #1)
2. Juan Antonio Luján, Indian, carpenter, fifty years old; married to Teresa Mirabal, *coyota*, thirty-five years old; two sons, ages sixteen and three; four daughters, ages twenty, eighteen, twelve, and four (family #41)
3. Leonor González, female Spaniard, widow, forty years old; two sons, ages twenty and sixteen; a female Indian servant of the Apache nation, sixteen years old (family #191)
4. The Lieutenant Don Vicente Armijo, Spaniard, breeder (*criador*), fifty-five years old; married to Casilda Chávez, female Spaniard, thirty-five years old; seven sons, one sixteen years old, another fourteen, another twelve, another ten, another eight, another six, another four; Indian servants: one female of the Apache nation, nineteen years old; another female Apache, nine years old; another *mestiza* servant, thirty-five years old; and another *mestiza*, fourteen years old (13 people in all) (family #249)
5. Doña Polonia Baca, female Spaniard, widow, fifty-three years old; one daughter, eighteen years old; one granddaughter, Spaniard, seven years old; one male Indian servant, seven years old; three female Indian servants: one of the Comanche nation, thirty-one years old; another of the Apache nation, thirty-six years old; another un-Christianized (*infiel*) of the Comanche nation, twenty-five years old (family #454)
6. Salvador Baca, Indian of the Apache nation, thirty-nine years old, day laborer; married to Ma del Carmen Herrera, female Spaniard, thirty-nine years old; two sons, one seventeen years old, another seven

years old; three daughters, one fifteen years old, another nine, another six (family #471)

From these six examples randomly selected one can learn that residents of Albuquerque included both married people (the majority) and widows and widowers, including one family headed by an Apache male married to a "Spanish" woman. The term *español* for Spaniard really meant anyone of Spanish heritage born in some place in New Spain, such as Mexico City. Such persons were often called Creoles elsewhere but not in the frontier community of Albuquerque. Furthermore, both males and females were listed as heads of households or families. Also, the presence of acculturated Apaches and Comanches in a Spanish community was quite common. Finally, large families were indicated with numbers of children by gender, indicating long years of childbearing and rearing. Occupations, as well as servitude, can also be obtained from the census.

Later censuses of New Mexico show that the population grew to 34,201 in 1793, with 29,041 of them in the three *villas* and other settlements of New Mexico proper and 5,160 at El Paso del Norte. Of the total, there were 22,851 Spaniards and mixed-bloods along with 11,350 Amerindians. Fortunately New Mexico, unlike Texas, had a detailed census report in 1817, reflecting 36,579 people in the province. Of these, 27,157 were Spaniards and mixed-bloods, while 9,422 Amerindians lived in the pueblos, in the Spanish settlements, and in *genízaro* villages composed of acculturated detribalized groups of Amerindians other than Pueblo Indians.[28] Thus the total population of New Mexico exceeded by three times those of Texas, Pimería Alta, and Alta California combined. Population totals are only one facet of the census returns that are valuable for study by various academic disciplines. Intensive examination of the *padrones* reveals other demographic information concerning dispersal and concentration of people; age structure of society; numbers of men, women, and children; ratios of men to women; marital status; numbers of widows and widowers; occupations and origins; classes of society; family sizes; servants and slaves; and relatives and orphans living within individual families. Studied across the decades from the earlier censuses of the late 1700s to those available around 1820, these examples of the Spanish written word reflect intrinsic information about human activity in the Greater Southwest. In addition, they show the changing nature of the human element on the frontiers.

Although maps, charts, sketches, plans, and censuses are important primary sources of information concerning the Greater Southwest and changing images of the region, they are not the only surviving materials of the Spanish word. Far from it! So too are diaries, journals, reports, and letters. These are numerous and often lengthy first-hand accounts concerning the nature, conditions, problems, and suggestions for reforms of the northern frontiers of New Spain. They contain information on administration, economies, societies, social customs, settlements, defense, military campaigns and policies, flora and fauna, explorations and discoveries, people, and especially Amerindian cultures encountered by the Spaniards. Although these documents provide valuable information, they must be studied with caution because of their exaggerations, contradictions, inaccuracies, and biases reflecting the views of their writers. Yet, one can derive some understanding from written descriptions of clothing worn by the *paisanos* (everyday people) of the frontiers, their housing and furnishings, conduct of ceremonies, recreations and diversions, crimes and punishments, occupations, and economic pursuits.

Municipal and provincial documents provided information on the everyday lives of settlers, both urban and rural. Records of the community of San Agustín de Laredo, founded in 1755 and then part of Nuevo Santander (now a part of Texas), are abundant and descriptive. They showed land grant procedures; surveying practices, town founding, and allotment of lands; mining, agricultural, and pastoral activities; educational efforts; local restrictions and laws; and customs of the people. For example, Laredo's parish priest objected to the mixed bathing of men and women in the Río Grande in 1784 as a poor example for children and an offense against "both majesties." His concerns resulted in a municipal law announced by the town's chief justice prohibiting heads of families from allowing their daughters to bathe with any men, even their brothers, although married men could do so with their wives if not accompanied by other men. Specific hours and days for bathing were also prescribed for each gender separately.[29] Local regulations in Laredo also governed the manufacture, introduction, and sale of liquor and attempted to regulate gambling, both widespread customs in Laredo and other frontier communities. Other municipal laws were issued at Laredo to regulate the slaughtering of cattle, carrying of firearms, and obtaining passports or licenses to travel outside of the community. These laws also controlled the visits of residents without a license to the nearby Carrizo Indian village to trade, obtain Amerindian servants, and mistreat its natives.[30]

These regulations not only revealed properties, customs, and practices of the inhabitants, but they showed the changing nature of society from an unregulated beginning to a more sophisticated, advanced, and controlled (perhaps "civilized") existence on the frontier. Likewise, two recent studies of an official on the one hand and visitors on the other illustrate not only the conditions of the time and place but the changing images of frontiers in the Greater Southwest.

The report of José Cortés, a lieutenant in the Royal Corps of Engineers stationed at Janos presidio in northern Chihuahua in 1799, concentrated upon describing the interior provinces of New Spain at the end of the eighteenth century, the presidios and their troops, and especially the Apaches, with whom the Spaniards were at war. Sympathetic to the Amerindians, the report also examined the threat from the United States to Spain's dominions in the Greater Southwest. "They love peace and hate to lose it," Cortés observed of the Apaches, who he thought practiced hunting and stealing because they had no other means of providing for themselves.[31] He also emphasized their important services as auxiliaries and *indios de paz* (peaceful Amerindians in settlements after 1786) to the Spanish defense of the northern frontier and noted that Apaches were the "first to fight as lions."[32] In the second part of his report, Cortés described the lands occupied or traversed by Apache bands and other tribal groups; Apache beliefs, superstitions, and marriages; their languages, dwellings, food, and nutrition; clothing; Apache agriculture and trade; leadership; hunting; weapons and methods of warfare; and finally their customs concerning death, mourning, and funerals.[33] The observations of Lieutenant Cortés about Apache customs and practices, together with his comments about other Amerindian cultures both east and west of the Río Grande,[34] provided one of the best detailed sources concerning the ethnohistory of Amerindians on the frontier. Also, Cortés's account indicated the changing images of Apaches from the earlier ones describing them as savages or *indios bárbaros* to a more objective analysis of their cultural traits and their usefulness as auxiliaries in warfare against other Apache and Amerindian enemies.

Illustrative of the value of such reports and reflective of the changing views of Spaniards toward the Greater Southwest was the visit of two naval officers, Dionisio Alcalá Galiano and Cayetano Valdéz, with the schooners *Sutil* and *Mexicana* to the coast of California in 1792. Following their reconnaissance of the northwest coast and Vancouver Island, they stopped at Monterey, California, and wrote in their journal an account of the visit. In this manuscript—now located in the Museo Naval in Madrid and discovered by Donald Cutter—Alcalá Galiano and Valdéz described the port of Monterey, its products and plants, the presidio, the mission of San Carlos Borromeo, and especially two Amerindian tribes, the Runsien (or Rumsen) and the Eslen (or Esselen). They provided information on the customs of the Runsien and Eslen peoples, one of the few sources describing these cultures, which soon after their visit would become extinct. The report also contained a catechism taught to the Amerindians at the mission of San Carlos and included a dictionary with Spanish equivalents of their words.[35] Although some of the naval officers' comments criticized the stupidity, laziness, and ugliness of the natives, they also noted that the Runsiens and Eslens were quick to learn and that they "cultivate the field, they care for the livestock, they make bricks, they build buildings, they make tools, works of carpentry, and so on."[36] Alcalá Galiano and Valdéz furthermore described the natives' hunting practices, dwellings of stone or adobe covered with branches of straw, occupations, clothing, methods of conversion to Christianity, and customs and religious ideas.[37] This report both provides a descriptive analysis of the Monterey area and its presidio, mission, and Amerindians at one time and serves as an important link in examining the changing nature of society in Spanish California between its beginnings in 1769–70 and the end of Spanish rule in 1821–22.

From other documents, such as church records, one learns about births, marriages, deaths, funerals, baptisms, and other details of frontier families. With such information about everyday persons, images of the colonial period cannot be reduced to the activities of explorers, conquistadores, civil officials, and religious leaders, both missionary and secular. Although such notables are valid figures to study, they comprised the minority, not the majority, of people settling and living on frontiers from Zacatecas to northern New Spain over the course of nearly three centuries.

As an illustration, one learns that women and children also were full participants in frontier history. Women had certain rights, such as becoming heads of households, initiating court proceedings, owning property, and having a role and voice in community affairs. Contrary to scholarly and popular opinion, both males and females populated the northern frontiers of New Spain, including those of the Greater Southwest. Though few if any women participated in exploratory ventures, a handful of them accompanied the colonizing force of Juan de Oñate to New Mexico in 1598, for example. Later, women were among the first settlers of Texas, and they soon came to California after its occupation in 1769–70. They bore children, the first ones usually during their teens, and afterward reared large families. Women owned property and usually inherited material assets upon their husbands' deaths. Furthermore, in New Mexico they regularly sought redress of grievances before the law with appeals or petitions to the governor or legal officials beginning with the phrase *pido y suplico* (I beseech and implore).[38] Decisions based upon law and necessity were rendered on such complaints as defamation of character, inheritance, and physical abuse by husbands.

Thus the law protected women, especially in property ownership. They inherited part of their parents' goods to use and will to heirs as they wished. When married, a woman continued to control this property unless she legally allowed her husband access to it. When her husband died, the widow was entitled to one-half of all goods acquired during the marriage with the remainder divided among her other heirs.[39] An example of a prominent New Mexican woman's estate is that of Juana Luján, who died in 1763, after making a will, a common practice among females. In it Luján, who lived near Santa Cruz de la Cañada, bequeathed her residence (a *rancho*, or small farm), lands, gardens, animals, tools, religious images, ceramics, textiles, personal items, and debts, which were to be paid by her executor.[40]

The participation of women as settlers and residents of Spanish communities, therefore, was also indicative of their changing numbers and roles in the society of the Greater Southwest. Although they may have been few in number in the initial settlements of Texas and New Mexico, there were thousands of them by the late eighteenth century in both provinces, as well as hundreds in Alta California and Pimería Alta. Their presence and rights should also cause today's scholars and the public to change their image of Spanish society as an all-male one that ignored the numbers and rights of women on Spanish frontiers. Just as women changed society on these frontiers, today's writers should alter their views of Spanish society to include women as an important segment of the population.

Often little appreciated by historians are official reports on Amerindians by civil officials, military officers, and ecclesiastics on the northern frontiers of New Spain. As introduced earlier for California, these observations changed over time. From the simple descriptions of Amerindian friends and enemies in the mid-sixteenth century, usually based upon insufficient knowledge and lack of objectivity, Spaniards rendered more complex reports with greater thoroughness and less bias by the mid-seventeenth century. Especially in the latter half of the eighteenth century and the early years of the nineteenth, these reports contained extensive information about both Christianized natives and unconverted tribal and band groups. Furthermore, they exhibited both positive and negative evaluations of the Amerindians and often objectively criticized Spanish settlers and military officers for their mistreatment of the natives. This ethnographic reportage, as Elizabeth A. H. John has recently observed, also "exemplifies a venerable legacy of the Spanish colonial frontier."[41]

A few examples will appropriately illustrate the changing views of Spaniards toward Amerindians on the frontiers of northern New Spain, including those of the Greater Southwest. Referring to the Chichimeca bands (Guachichiles, Zacatecos, Guamares, and Pames) of the Zacatecas frontier between 1550 and 1600, Spaniards portrayed the typical Amerindian as a "dirty, uncivilized dog."[42] This epithet, acquired from other Amerindians in the area of central Mexico after the conquest by Hernán Cortés, demonstrated the contempt both Aztec allies and Spaniards felt for the Chichimecas: their barbarity, their nudity, and their customs. While describing the hairstyles of the Chichimecas, their painting of faces and bodies, their dwellings, dietary habits, methods of warfare, and their enslavement of and cruelty toward captives, Spaniards also focused upon Chichimeca primitiveness in religion and social organization. Yet they praised their enemies for their tactics, bravery, resistance, and defense of property, while denouncing their "savagery," thievery, arrogance, audacity, and "barbarous" nature.[43] This gave rise to the commonly used phrase *indios bárbaros* so widely practiced then and thereafter to describe hostile, unconverted Amerindian nations, tribes, and bands.

In the mid-seventeenth century Licenciado Diego de Medrano, a priest in the city of Durango, capital of the kingdom of Nueva Vizcaya, wrote a lengthy report describing the "riots and ruin wrought by the rebellious Indians."[44] This document and its revision in 1660 advised the viceroy of New Spain and the archbishop of México about frontier defense. It also detailed the history of Spanish-Indian conflicts in the kingdom during the first half of the seventeenth century. Furthermore, it examined the customs, beliefs, and practices of enemy Amerindians. Medrano noted that the causes of rebellions by Acaxees, Xiximes, Tepehuanes, Tobosos, Tarahumares, Salineros, Conchos, and Cabezas "can be found in the instability and inconsistency of the Indian temperament, their thievish and innately cruel nature, and their great hatred of Spaniards," influenced by their shamans, who were "instruments of the devil" and incited their listeners to "rebel and commit atrocities."[45]

Although this ethnocentric observation blamed the Indians, Medrano also noted that the Acaxee rebellion resulted from the "bad treatment the Indians received in the mining haciendas of San Andrés."[46] With perception, understanding, and the ability to distinguish one Amerindian nation from another, he singled out the Tarahumares for praise as the "most courteous, peaceable, pacific, and industrious nation in the kingdom." Medrano detailed their agricultural and pastoral pursuits, the fact that they wore clothes, their docility, and that they did not engage in raids. The Tarahumares had not murdered a single person or stolen a single animal, were honest and punctual, and even in warfare against the Spaniards did not practice treachery or ambush but instead met the Spaniards in battle at an appointed time and place. He blamed greedy Spaniards for buying maize from the Tarahumares to sell at inflated prices in Parral, thus making bread too expensive for the poor; and other Spaniards for enslaving and mistreating Tarahumar women and children, thereby justifying the Amerindians in their wars because they "have sought only to defend themselves."[47] Such comments revealed the changing attitudes of some Spaniards toward the Amerindians of northern New Spain and the Greater Southwest.

Even more so were the views reflected in the reports of clergy and civil officials during the late eighteenth and early nineteenth centuries. For example, Father Ignaz Pfefferkorn, a Jesuit missionary in Sonora in 1767, described in detail the various Amerindian nations and tribes of Sonora, including both friendly, Christianized ones (the Opatas, Pimas, and Eudebes) and the "wild" Apaches and Seris. Although his observations occasionally preserved the older attitudes toward the natives and showed his own ethnocentric beliefs, most of his comments objectively described the natives' modes of living, houses, food, utensils, occupations, superstitions, languages, and religious beliefs and practices. "The Apaches are the most modest Indians in New Spain," he wrote, because they "were never seen naked."[48]

Father Pfefferkorn went on to point out that the Apaches were monogamous and abhorred adultery, which they punished by tying the adulterer to a tree and shooting him with arrows, while the guilty woman had her nose cut off as a symbol of eternal disgrace. Apaches, according to the Jesuit, acknowledged no leader to obey and be their judge except on campaigns; in general each Apache was "his own master and in every way lives according to his own pleasure." In addition, he described Apache dwellings as "poor huts built of tree branches, covered over with foliage"; their habit of sleeping on the bare earth; and their planting of maize, beans, and gourds in such small quantities that they had to raid, rob, and steal to prevent starvation. The Apaches were "incomparable archers and seldom miss," he noted, and the force of their arrows had "more power and effectiveness than a bullet from the best musket." Describing their plundering expeditions, methods of warfare, and treatment of captives, he concluded that they were "fierce, hereditary enemies" whom he sometimes called "savages."[49]

Yet he also overgeneralized about Amerindians by stating that "there is so little difference among the native Americans . . . that he who has seen one American can almost say that he has seen them all" because of their chestnut brown color, bodily structure, disposition, passions, and manners and customs.[50] Although he also criticized Spaniards for their wickedness toward and mistreatment of Sonoran Amerindians,[51] Father Pfefferkorn criticized even the friendly Amerindians for their preoccupation with the present, lack of kindness and sympathy, animal instincts, stupidity, indolence, thievery, disorderly living, and lack of religion.[52] "Their want of knowledge about God," he wrote, "originated partly from their pitiable stupidity and inability to arrive at reasonable conclusions, and partly from their animal-like existence which suppressed all reason. In some cases wickedness was also responsible."[53] Yet, in his overall evaluation of Sonoran Amerindians, he excepted the Christian Opatas and Eudebes, whom he praised for the "improvement of their customs."[54]

Military and civilian officials during the late colonial period rendered reports that were increasingly dispassionate, objective, and understanding of Amerindian nations and tribes. In addition, their perceptiveness demonstrated the changing views of Spaniards toward both friendly and hostile natives. Although there were many such reports from the mid-1760s to the early 1800s, their nature concerning Apaches, for example, was reflected in the careful studies of two military officers—Commandant Inspector Antonio Cordero y Bustamante in 1796[55] and Lieutenant José Cortés in 1799[56]—and one civilian bureaucrat, Manuel Merino y Moreno, about 1804.

Merino, who was nearing the end of his service as secretary of the archives of the commandant-general in Chihuahua, composed a lengthy report expressing considerable knowledge of Apaches on the northern frontier.[57] Using data from Cordero's earlier report in addition to his own observations and familiarity with reports in the archives, Merino described both hostile Apaches and those in *establecimientos de paz* (peace settlements).[58] He wisely did not overgeneralize about all Apaches, describing nine principal groups or bands: Tontos, Chiricagues, Gileños, Mimbreños, Faraones, Mescaleros, Llaneros, Lipanes, and Nabajoes. "Today they do not constitute a uniform nation in their customs, habits, and preferences," he wrote, although they did speak a common language but with differences of accent and vocabulary.[59] Merino went on to describe objectively the character of Apaches as "astute, distrustful, bold, and haughty," being very "zealous of their freedom and independence." Praising their hardiness, movement from one *ranchería* (temporary camp) to another, agility, and quickness, he also described the dress of the men and women, Apache polygamy, and the size and nature of their *rancherías* as well as their circular huts, or *jacales*, and their foods.[60] His report also explained their dances (their favorite entertainment), hunting methods, weapons (lances, bows, arrows, and some firearms possessed by the Mescaleros and Lipanes), their alleged propensity for stealing and violence, and their use of smoke signals for communication.[61] Of special note is the fact that Merino described the religious beliefs of Apaches in neutral terms except for one instance of calling them barbarians.[62]

Within his report, Merino also referred to Tontos residing in *establecimientos de paz* near Tucson and Chiricahuas living at the village of Bacuachi in Sonora and the presidio of Janos in Chihuahua.[63] Although he noted the presence of some Mescaleros formerly settled in peace near the presidio of La Junta de los Ríos (Presidio del Norte), he observed that they had broken the peace "treacherously" and returned to their country.[64] Unfortunately this part of the report is misleading. Although some Mescaleros did indeed abandon La Junta de los Ríos after 1795, about one-third of them remained loyal to the Spaniards and stayed in the region, accepting Christianity and becoming part of the racially mixed population through baptism and acculturation.[65] In summary, Merino's report reflected new attitudes and views toward Apaches, along with observations about Navajos, Comanches, Yumas, Papagos, Pimas, and Hopis. It also contained some information about the Amerindians of Texas, although this material was less thorough and accurate.[66]

It should not be concluded that the Spanish written word was solely

Fig. 3. The Spanish translated features of the New World into their written language and their graphic vocabulary, as seen in this image of a buffalo from Gómara, *La Historia de las Indias*, 1553. (Author's collection.)

restricted to changing descriptions of and views toward Amerindians. Reports and letters contained extensive observations about the geographical extent of the developing frontier, physical features, climates, founding of towns, population, society, occupations and economic pursuits, defense, military and ecclesiastical matters, foods, dwellings, flora, and fauna.

Spanish descriptions of strange animals began with Francisco de Garay's expedition of 1523 to the region of today's Soto la Marina in Tamaulipas. They continued with the trek of Alvar Núñez Cabeza de Vaca and the expeditions of Francisco Vázquez de Coronado and Juan de Oñate, all before 1600. When one of Garay's exploring parties returned to the Río de las Palmas, it brought back an armadillo, which was taken aboard one of the ships where it later died. When captured, the armadillo was described as a "quadruped, a little larger than a cat, with the face of a wolf, silver colored, scaly, and caparisoned as the armed cuirasser going into battle caparisons his horse. A sluggish creature it folded itself up like a hedgehog or a tortoise on seeing a man at a distance and allowed itself to be caught."[67] In this manner Spaniards tried to describe a new animal of the northern frontier by resorting to descriptions of other animals familiar to Europeans.

Similarly, Spaniards tried to describe the bison (fig. 3) they encountered in the Greater Southwest, with varying and changing portrayals. Cabeza de Vaca, in the latter part of his journey across southern Texas in 1535–36, called bison "cattle" and reported having seen and eaten them on three occasions. "I think they are about the size of those in Spain," he wrote. "They have small horns like the cows of Morocco; their hair is very long and flocky like merinos. Some are tawny and others black. In my opinion the meat is finer and fatter than the beef of this country [Spain]. The Indians make blankets of the skins of cows not full grown; and shoes and shields from the full grown," and the natives traded an "incredible number of their hides into the interior."[68] Seven years later, Pedro de Castañeda, chronicler of the Coronado expedition, which saw great numbers of bison on today's Great Plains of eastern New Mexico and western Texas, also described these animals. Calling them "cattle," Castañeda explained that

> their faces are shorter and narrow between the eyes, the forehead two spans wide. Their eyes bulge out on the side, so that when they run they can see anyone who follows them. They are bearded like large goats, and when they run they carry their heads low, their beards touching the ground. From the middle of the body toward the rear they are covered with very fine woolly hair like that of a choice sheep, and from the belly forward they have thick hair like the mane of a wild lion. They have a hump larger than that of a camel, and their horns, which barely show through the hair, are short and thick. During May they shed the hair on the rear half of the body, and then they look exactly like lions. To remove the hair they lean against small trees found in some of the gorges and rub against them until they shed the wool, as a snake sheds its skin. They have a short tail with a small bunch of hair at the end, and when they run they carry it erect like a scorpion. One peculiar thing is that when they are calves they are reddish like ours, but in time, as they become older, they change color and appearance. Furthermore, all the bulls slaughtered had their left ears slit, although when they are calves they are whole.[69]

Castañeda also explained that bison hides, usually of dark red wool, could be made into garments and that the animals ranged in large herds over a distance of more than forty leagues (about one hundred and five miles).[70] Once again it is evident that Castañeda, like Cabeza de Vaca, had tried to explain the appearance of bison to those unfamiliar with the animal in terms they could understand. Furthermore, he emphasized that the *Querecho* (Apache?) Indians lived in tents made of the tanned skins of the "cows" and that they used the flesh of the bison for making dried beef (pemmican) seasoned with animal fat. They drank the animal's blood from a large gut that was emptied and filled, which they carried about the neck to drink when they were thirsty.[71]

With such vivid descriptions of the bison, other Spaniards, without having seen one, tried to depict the animal in sketches and drawings. As an example, Francisco López de Gómara, who published his *Historia general de las Indias* in the early 1550s, included a sketch of a bison as he imagined it from the early descriptions of those who had seen it.[72] Though not very realistic, this portrait gave Europeans their first visual idea of the physical appearance of a bison.

Thereafter, Spaniards continued their fascination with and efforts to describe bison for the benefit of those in Spain. Juan de Oñate, who settled New Mexico in 1598 and explored the Great Plains following the initial colonization, reported having seen one hundred thousand of them in what is today's western Texas. He explained that "they are cattle, terribly obstinate, courageous beyond exaggeration, and so cunning that if pursued, they run, and that if their pursuers stop or slacken their speed, they stop and roll, just like mules and with this respite renew their run." Bison evidently charged Oñate's force, killing three of his horses and injuring forty others. "Their horns are very sharp and fairly long, about a span and a half, and bent upward together. They attack from the side, putting the head far down, so that whatever they seize they tear very badly," he explained. Observing that the meat and tallow of the bison were very good,[73] Oñate went on to describe the animal as follows:

> Its shape and form are so marvelous and laughable, or frightful, that the more one sees it the more one desires to see it, and no one could be so melancholy that if he were to see it a hundred times a day he could [not] keep from laughing heartily as many times, or could fail to marvel at the sight of so ferocious an animal. Its horns are black and a third of a *vara* [about eleven inches] long . . . and resemble those of a *búfalo* [Asiatic buffalo]; its eyes are small, its face, snout, feet, and hoofs of the same form as our cows with the exception that both the male and female are very much bearded, similar to he goats. They are so thickly covered with wool that it covers their eyes and face and the forelock nearly envelops their horns. Their wool, which is long and very soft, extends almost to the middle of the body, but from there on the hair is shorter. Over the ribs they have so much wool and the chine is so high that they appear to be hump-backed, although in reality and truth they are not greatly so, for the hump easily disappears when the hides are stretched. In general, they are larger than our cattle. Their tail is like that of a hog, being very short, and having few bristles at the tip, and they twist it upward when they run. At the knee they have natural garters of

very long hair. [They run] in leaps, especially downhill. They are all of the same dark color, somewhat tawny, in parts their hair being almost black.[74]

Oñate concluded that bison were more "ferocious than the pen can depict,"[75] an observation common to all Spaniards who saw them. Nearly three-quarters of a century later in 1675, Fernando del Bosque, who journeyed from Coahuila into southern Texas and killed three bulls and two cows for food, described the meat and appearance of the bison as follows:

> The meat is very savory. The form of the buffalo is very ugly. Although large, they resemble cows and bulls. Their hair is very shaggy. The withers are very high, making them appear humpbacked, and their necks are very large. The head is short and very shaggy, so that the wool covers the eyes and prevents them from seeing well. The horns are small and thick, but like those of the bull. The hips and haunches are like those of a hog, and the tail is bare except at the end, where there are long bristles. The hoofs are cloven, and at the knees from there up the shoulder there is much bristlelike hair, like he goats. The females are of the same sort, and have four teats. They gaze at the people sidewise like wild hogs, with hair abristle.[76]

From these descriptions of the bison, one can glean much information about an animal of the Greater Southwest that was new and strange to Europeans. Although there are some contradictions among these descriptions, there are also common aspects. The reports of such Spaniards provide information for research, as well as depict changing views of Spaniards toward one of the most novel animals of the region we call the Greater Southwest.

The Spanish written word also presented views about plants, trees, and food found in the region and often consumed by the Amerindians. Cabeza de Vaca, for example, mentioned foods found in southern Texas: fish, roots, oysters, blackberries, and especially prickly pears from the cactus. The latter he described as "the size of a hen's egg, bright red and black in color, and good tasting," enabling the natives to live solely on its fruit and juice for three months each year.[77] More than two centuries later and on another frontier in Sonora, Jesuit Father Pfefferkorn furnished a tasty description of chile peppers. When the peppers were still green, Sonorans roasted them to remove the outer skin, which was perceived to be too hot to the taste. They then ate the peppers with such appetite that their mouths frothed and tears came to their eyes, proclaiming the chile pepper to be "a very healthful and cooling dish," according to the missionary. Another custom he described for the use of the peppers was to pick them when the fruit was red, black, or brown and completely ripe, string them, and hang them up to dry.[78] This has become a popular custom of today's *ristras.* If not eaten whole or hung up to dry, chile peppers were also used to prepare sauces, as described by Pfefferkorn. "No dish is more agreeable to an American, but to a foreigner it is intolerable, especially at first, because of the monotonous hotness of the peppers. The constant use of this hot sauce is at first an unbelievable hardship for the European. He must be content with either dry bread or burn his tongue and gums, as I did when, after a difficult fifteen-hour journey, I tried for the first time to still my hunger with such a dish. After the first mouthful the tears started to come. I could not say a word and believed I had hell-fire in my mouth. However, one becomes accustomed to it after frequent bold victories, so that with time the dish becomes tolerable and finally very agreeable."[79]

Within these descriptions of animals and foods one finds examples not only of creatures, diets, and different nutritional aspects of the changing frontiers of New Spain but changing views of the Greater Southwest. It is especially notable that in the latter half of the eighteenth century, Father Pfefferkorn used the term *American*. This word was never used in Cabeza de Vaca's sixteenth century but was becoming more commonly employed in the Spanish spoken and written word during the last years of Spain's hegemony in the New World.

Indicative also of changing views of the Greater Southwest expressed in various forms of the Spanish written word is evidence from scientific expeditions to Alta California and the northwestern coast of North America in the last quarter of the eighteenth century. Alejandro Malaspina and the Royal Scientific Expedition of New Spain conducted such excursions in the late 1780s, and throughout the 1790s the journeys included scientists and artists. José Mariano Moziño, a thirty-year-old Mexican-born scientist with the royal expedition, conducted a scientific survey of Nootka Sound on Vancouver Island and compiled a thorough ethnographic study of its native inhabitants as well as the flora and fauna of the island. Talented artist Atanasio Echeverría worked with Moziño and carefully sketched and painted illustrations of birds, butterflies, fish, bats, reptiles, animals, and plants.[80]

Another scientist, Tadeo Haenke of Bohemian birth, accompanied the Malaspina expedition, as did José Cardero and Tomás de Suría. In the Pacific Northwest and California they examined Amerindian customs and drew sketches of botanical and zoological features, geographical diagrams of coasts and bays, and portraits of Amerindians. Cardero also accompanied the expedition of Dionisio Alcalá Galiano and Cayetano Valdéz to California and the Pacific Northwest with the schooners *Sutil* and *Mexicana* in 1792. His records from the two voyages depicted general scenes, native types, zoological and botanical observations accompanied by illustrations, and details about the native cultures.[81] With remarkable clarity and scientific analysis, Moziño, Haenke, Cardero, and Suría, among others, demonstrated the concepts of The Enlightenment. Their views, both in writing and in the arts, reflected more detailed and accurate portrayals of the Pacific coastal region of the Greater Southwest and changing views of the native people, geography, flora, and fauna in the last years of Spain's experience in this vast region. Furthermore, these forms of the written word contrasted greatly with the earlier ones of the preceding centuries.

The historical frontiers of northern New Spain included the region of the Greater Southwest and were ever-changing and dynamic, not static. By 1600 the frontiers had reached Nueva Vizcaya as far as southern Chihuahua, portions of Coahuila, and the settlement of isolated New Mexico. One hundred years later Spanish expansion had reached Sonora (including Pimería Alta in today's southern Arizona), Baja California, El Paso del Norte, and Nuevo León. The Spanish had also established temporary mission communities in eastern Texas, which failed in 1693. By 1800 the frontiers of the Greater Southwest had been reached with the occupation of Texas; Nuevo Santander (today's Tamaulipas); the central and northern parts of Chihuahua at Chihuahua City and Janos presidio; Tucson in Pimería Alta; new settlements, such as Albuquerque, in New Mexico; the occupation of Alta California; and temporary settlements at Neah Bay in the state of Washington and at Nootka Sound on Vancouver Island. Both of the latter settlements were abandoned by Spain in 1792 and 1795, respectively.

In this process of expansion, conquest and colonization followed exploration, mostly in a northward direction but occasionally filling in areas to the south of previously existing northern regions. In all of these areas Spanish officials and settlers encountered Amerindians. Some of them were subjugated by warfare, but many of them had been pacified by other means and acculturated to European life-styles by the 1790s. By that time some former frontiers, such as Durango, had passed beyond the frontier stage, but most of the area of the Greater Southwest existed as the *frontera septentrional* (northernmost frontier) of New Spain. It was still remote, isolated, and threatened by hostile Amerindians and foreign nations, although peaceful arrangements with some Apaches, Comanches, Utes, and Navajos had lessened the threat of hostile natives in Texas and New Mexico, as well as in northern Chihuahua and Sonora.

Although this study has examined the Spanish written word in various forms inscribed on paper, it should also be noted that written language appeared in at least one instance on the rock of El Morro (Inscription Rock) in western New Mexico between Zuñi Pueblo and the Río Grande with this message: "Paso por aqui el adelantado don Juan de Onate del descubrimiento de la mar del sur a 16 de abril de 1605." (Passed by here the Governor General Don Juan de Oñate from the discovery of the South Sea on April 16, 1605.)[82] This historically important graffiti of the early seventeenth century informs us that Governor Juan de Oñate used this route on the way back to New Mexico from the Gulf of California (the "South Sea"), returning to the town of San Gabriel de los Españoles on April 25, 1605.

Changing Spanish images and views of the frontier were expressed in a variety of written or literary forms over the course of centuries. These evolving images of geography, Amerindians, life-styles, population, flora, and fauna were recorded in governmental and ecclesiastical reports, diaries and journals, maps and charts, censuses, and personal correspondence. They are all still available in archival and library repositories in Spain, Mexico, the United States, and elsewhere.

What Cristóbal Colón set in motion with encounter and change for the Caribbean islands, his successors continued in northern New Spain, a region Colón never reached, and elsewhere in the Americas. The Spanish written word is often the only surviving source of information and record for the Greater Southwest in the colonial era extending over nearly three centuries before Mexican independence. As such, the written word of the Spaniards has often been taken for granted, neglected, or ignored, but it constitutes an important part of the legacy of Spain to America.

NOTES

1. Throughout this study the author uses the term *America* for all of the Western Hemisphere, not just the United States of America.

2. For example, Alfred W. Crosby, *The Columbian Exchange: Biological and Cultural Consequences of 1492* (Westport, Conn.: Greenwood Press, 1972); Mark A. Burkholder and

Lyman L. Johnson, *Colonial Latin America* (New York and Oxford: Oxford University Press, 1990), pp. 60–67.

3. Burkholder and Johnson, *Colonial Latin America*, p. 67; Noble D. Cook and W. George Lovell, eds., *"Secret Judgments of God": Old World Disease in Colonial Spanish America* (Norman: University of Oklahoma Press, 1991), pp. 11–12. Cook and Lovell's work is the most recent comprehensive account of the transmission of diseases between Europe and America in the colonial era. One of the best studies of the exchange of people, plants, animals, and products, examining both what was brought to America from Spain and what came from America to Europe, is the little-known and almost never cited J. Garcia Mercadel, *Lo que España llevó a América* (Madrid: Taurus Ediciones, 1959).

4. New Spain was the name given by Spaniards to present-day Mexico, the southwestern United States, Central America from Guatemala to Panama's border with Costa Rica, and the Philippine Islands. The Viceroyalty of New Spain was created in 1535 and endured until Mexico's independence from Spain in September, 1821. Panama was not a part of New Spain for most of the period. It was first a part of the Viceroyalty of Peru and during most of the eighteenth century was included in the Viceroyalty of Nueva Granada.

5. Center for Greater Southwestern Studies and the History of Cartography, the University of Texas at Arlington, *Fronteras* 1, no. 1 (Spring, 1992): 1–2. Defining the region of the Southwest and the Greater Southwest has long been a controversial topic among scholars and the public. For differing definitions, see Oakah L. Jones, "The Borderlands after Bolton and Bannon: A Southwest View" (paper presented at the Annual Meeting of the Western History Association, Los Angeles, Calif., Oct. 10, 1987).

6. See, for example, on Spain at Nootka and Núñez Gaona, Oakah L. Jones, "The Spanish Occupation of Nootka Sound, 1790–1795" (master's thesis, University of Oklahoma, 1960); and on the Pacific and Northwest Coasts of North America, Warren L. Cook, *Flood Tide of Empire: Spain and the Pacific Northwest, 1543–1819* (New Haven: Yale University Press, 1973).

7. Thomas H. Naylor and Charles W. Polzer, S.J., comps. and eds., *The Presidio and the Militia on the Northern Frontier of New Spain: A Documentary History. Volume One: 1570–1700* (Tucson: University of Arizona Press, 1986), p. 4.

8. For the legacy of Spain to the history of the United States, especially the Southwest and the Southeast (from Florida to Louisiana), see David J. Weber, "The Spanish Legacy in North America and the Historical Imagination," *Western Historical Quarterly* 23, no. 1 (Feb., 1992): 5–24; and Weber, *The Spanish Frontier in North America* (New Haven: Yale University Press, 1992), chap. 12, pp. 335–60. See also Donald E. Worcester, "The Significance of the Spanish Borderlands to the United States," *Western Historical Quarterly* 7, no. 1 (Jan., 1976): 279–93; Gerald E. Poyo and Gilberto M. Hinojosa, "Spanish Texas and Borderlands Historiography in Transition: Implications for United States History," *Journal of American History* 75, no. 2 (Sept., 1988): 393–416; and Donald C. Cutter, "The Western Spanish Borderlands," in Michael P. Malone, ed., *Historians and the American West* (Lincoln: University of Nebraska Press, 1983), pp. 39–56.

9. Elizabeth A. H. John has recently published an important article emphasizing the exhaustive and numerous reports of Spaniards concerning Amerindians written by Herbert E. Bolton and later Spanish Borderlands historians. See John, "A View from the Spanish Borderlands," *Proceedings of the American Antiquarian Society* 101, pt. 1 (1991): 77–87.

10. Harry Kelsey, "Spanish Entrada Cartography" (paper presented at the symposium of "After Columbus: The Spanish Legacy in the Southwest," the Huntington Library, San Marino, Calif., May 15, 1992), p. 1.

11. Ibid., pp. 2, 32.

12. Mapa de Nueva Vizcaya, 1667, Archivo General de Indias, Mapas y Planos, México, 615; Oakah L. Jones, Jr., *Nueva Vizcaya: Heartland of the Spanish Frontier* (Albuquerque: University of New Mexico Press, 1988), pp. 32–33, 106.

13. Ernest J. Burrus, S.J., *Kino and the Cartography of Northwestern New Spain* (Tucson: Arizona Pioneers' Historical Society, 1965), pp. 13, 14.

14. Thomas H. Naylor and Charles W. Polzer, S.J., comps. and eds., *Pedro de Rivera and the Military Regulations for Northern New Spain, 1724–1729: A Documentary History of His Frontier Inspection and the Reglamento de 1729* (Tucson: University of Arizona Press, 1988).

15. For the inspection of Rubi and the map of Lafora, see Nicolás de Lafora, *Relación del viaje que hizo a los Presidios Internos situados en la Frontera de la América Septentrional perteneciente al Rey de España*, ed. Vito Alessio Robles (Mexico: Editorial Pedro Robredo, 1939); and Lawrence Kinnaird, ed., *The Frontiers of New Spain: Nicolás de Lafora's Description, 1766–1768*, vol. 13 of *Quivira Society Publications* (Berkeley: Quivira Society, 1958). See also Max L. Moorhead, *The Presidio: Bastion of the Spanish Borderlands* (Norman: University of Oklahoma Press, 1975), pp. 56–61.

16. Moorhead, *The Presidio*, pp. 56–57, and note 25.

17. For the Dominguez-Vélez de Escalante expedition, see Ted J. Warner, ed., *The Dominguez-Escalante Journal: Their Expedition through Colorado, Utah, Arizona, and New Mexico in 1776*, trans. Fray Angelico Chavez (Provo: Brigham Young University Press, 1976). It contains information about and portions of the map by Miera y Pacheco, as does Eleanor B. Adams and Fray Angelico Chavez, eds. and trans., *The Missions of New Mexico: A Description by Fray Francisco Atanasio Dominguez with other Contemporary Documents* (Albuquerque: University of New Mexico Press, 1956).

18. For these explorations and their maps and artists, see Henry Raup Wagner, *The Cartography of the Northwest Coast of North America to the Year 1800*, 2 vols. (Berkeley: University of California Press, 1937); Iris H. W. Engstrand, *Spanish Scientists in the New World* (Seattle: University of Washington Press, 1981); Iris Higbie Wilson, trans. and ed., *Noticias de Nutka: An Account of Nootka Sound in 1792 by José Mariano Moziño* (Seattle: University of Washington Press, 1970); Donald C. Cutter, *Malaspina in California* (San Francisco: John Howell Books, 1960); Donald C. Cutter, *California in 1792: A Spanish Naval Visit* (Norman: University of Oklahoma Press, 1990); and Cook, *Flood Tide of Empire*.

19. Burrus, *Kino and Cartography*, p. 13; Oakah L. Jones, commentary on Kelsey, "Spanish Entrada Cartography," pp. 1, 6–7.

20. Marín's inspection and report are in Charles W. Hackett, ed., *Historical Documents Relating to New Mexico, Nueva Vizcaya, and Approaches thereto, to 1773*, 3 vols. (Washington, D.C.: Carnegie Institution, 1923–37), vol. 2, pp. 387–409. For the Rivera inspection, see Naylor and Polzer, *Pedro de Rivera*, and Pedro de Rivera, *Diario y derrotero de lo caminado, visto y observado en el discurso de la visita general de los presidios situados en las provincias internas de Nueva España*, ed. Guillermo Porras Muñoz (México: Costa-Amic, 1945). For the inspection of the Marqués de Rubí, see citations in note 15. For reports of Bishop Tamarón y Romeral, see Vito Alessio Robles, ed., *Demostración del vastisimo obispado de la Nueva Vizcaya—1765* (México: Antigua Libreria Robredo de José Porrua e hijos, 1937); and Eleanor B. Adams, ed., *Bishop Tamarón's Visitation of New Mexico, 1760*, vol. 15 of Historical Society of New Mexico, *Publications in History* (Albuquerque, 1954). See also Jones, *Nueva Vizcaya*, pp. 109–13, 126–34, and 160–63.

21. El Barón de Ripperdá, "Estado general que manifiesta el número de vasallos y habitantes que tiene el Rey en esta Provincia de Texas . . . , Béjar," Nov. 6, 1777, Biblioteca Nacional de México, in Juan Agustín de Morfi, *Viaje de indios y diario del Nuevo México*, ed.

Vito Alessio Robles, 2d ed. (México: Antigua Libreria Robredo de José Porrúa e hijos, 1935), app. 2, pp. 275–80; Oakah L. Jones, Jr., *Los Paisanos: Spanish Settlers on the Northern Frontier of New Spain* (Norman: University of Oklahoma Press, 1979), p. 47.

22. Juan Bauta de Elguezábal, "Estado que manifiesta el número de habitantes en la dicha provincia en el año 1804, Provincia de Texas, San Antonio de Béxar," Jan. 30, 1805, Béxar Archives, University of Texas at Austin, B24/133; Nettie Lee Benson, ed. and trans., "A Governor's Report on Texas in 1809," *Southwestern Historical Quarterly* 71, no. 4 (Apr., 1968): 611; Jones, *Los Paisanos*, pp. 47–48.

23. "Real Presidio de la Bahia de el Espiritu Santo, Extracto general de la tropa y vecindario de dicho presidio, January 12, 1780" (Texas History Research Library, the Alamo, San Antonio, photocopy); Jones, *Los Paisanos*, pp. 48–50.

24. Bernardo Serña and Fr. The. Franco. López, "Padrón de almas que existen en 31 de diciembre de 1792," San Antonio de Béxar, Dec. 31, 1792, Nacogdoches Archives, Texas State Library, Austin.

25. Jones, *Los Paisanos*, p. 127. The 1790 census is in the Spanish Archives of New Mexico (hereafter SANM), State Records Center and Archives, Santa Fe, N.Mex., and in microcopy on reel 12, frames 319–53, 355–62, 372–407, 428, 459–62, 486–96, and 501–502.

26. Jones, *Los Paisanos*, p. 127. For a detailed examination of the 1790 census in New Mexico, see Oakah L. Jones, Jr., "Spanish Civil Communities and Settlers in Frontier New Mexico, 1790–1810," in William S. Coker, ed., *Hispanic American Essays in Honor of Max Leon Moorhead* (Pensacola: Perdido Bay Press, 1979), pp. 37–60. For the 1810 census, see Fr. Josef Benito Pereyra, "Noticia de las misiones que ocupan . . . dicha provincia de Nuevo México," Dec. 31, 1810, Ritch Collection, Huntington Library, San Marino, Calif., RI 68.

27. "Padrón General de esta Jurisdicción de la Alcaldia de Sn Phelipe de Albuquerque." Provincia del Nuevo México, 22 de Octubre de 1790, SANM, microcopy, reel 12, frames 319–53.

28. "Estado que manifiesta el número de vasallos y [h]avitantes," Santa Fe, N.Mex., Nov. 20, 1793, SANM, microcopy, reel 13, frame 428; "Estado que manifiesta el número de vasallos y habitantes, prova del Nuevo México," fin de diciembre de 1817, SANM, microcopy, reel 18, frame 870.

29. Santiago de Jesús Sánchez, Villa de San Agustín de Laredo, May 30, 1784, Laredo Archives, Saint Mary's University, San Antonio; Jones, *Los Paisanos*, p. 74. For an overall study of Laredo, see Gilberto M. Hinojosa, *A Borderlands Town in Transition: Laredo, 1755-1870* (College Station: Texas A&M University Press, 1983).

30. Jones, *Los Paisanos*, pp. 74–75, citing various documents from the Laredo Archives.

31. José Cortés, *Views from the Apache Frontier: Report on the Northern Provinces of New Spain*, ed. Elizabeth A. H. John, trans. John Wheat (Norman: University of Oklahoma Press, 1989), pp. xiii, 28.

32. Ibid., pp. 29, 30.

33. Ibid., pp. 49–79.

34. Ibid., pp. 81–109.

35. Cutter, *California in 1792.* The Runsien and Eslen Amerindians are discussed on p. 113, note 25, and pp. 132–50. The dictionary of their languages appears on pp. 147–49 and the catechism on pp. 151–55.

36. Ibid., pp. 132–33.

37. Ibid., pp. 133–34, 138, 139–50.

38. Rosalind Z. Rock, "'Pido y Suplico': Women and the Law in Spanish New Mexico, 1697–1763," *New Mexico Historical Review* 65, no. 2 (Apr., 1990): 145 and note 1. For a study of New Mexican women as settlers at the end of the seventeenth century, see Salome

Hernández, "Nueva [*sic*] Mexicanas as Refugees and Reconquest Settlers, 1680–1696," in Joan M. Jensen and Darlis Miller, eds., *New Mexico Women: Intercultural Perspectives* (Albuquerque: University of New Mexico Press, 1986).

39. Rock, "'Pido y Suplico,'" p. 148.

40. Richard E. Ahlborn,"The Will of a New Mexico Woman in 1762," *New Mexico Historical Review* 65, no. 3 (July, 1990): 327–30. App. C, pp. 341–55, lists the material items in Juana Luján's will and gives an inventory of them.

41. Elizabeth A. H. John, ed., "Views from a Desk in Chihuahua: Manuel Merino's Report on Apaches and Neighboring Nations, ca. 1804," trans. John Wheat, *Southwestern Historical Quarterly* 95 (Oct., 1991): 139.

42. Philip W. Powell, *Soldiers, Indians, and Silver: The Northward Advance of New Spain, 1550–1600* (Berkeley: University of California Press, 1952), p. 33.

43. Ibid., pp. 33–54. See also Philip W. Powell, "The Chichimecas: Scourge of the Silver Frontier in Sixteenth-Century Mexico," *Hispanic American Historical Review* 25 (Aug., 1945): 315–38.

44. "Relación de Diego Medrano, Durango, August 31, 1654," in Naylor and Polzer, eds., *The Presidio and the Militia*, pp. 409–11.

45. Ibid., pp. 412–13.

46. Ibid., p. 413.

47. Ibid., pp. 422–23.

48. Ignaz Pfefferkorn, *Sonora: A Description of the Province*, trans. and ed. Theodore E. Treutlein, vol. 12 of *Coronado Cuarto Centennial Publications, 1540–1940*, ed. George P. Hammond (Albuquerque: University of New Mexico Press, 1949), p. 145.

49. Ibid., pp. 144–50; "savages," p. 32.

50. Ibid., p. 163.

51. Ibid., pp. 32–36.

52. Ibid., pp. 166, 167, 168, 170, 174–89, 224.

53. Ibid., p. 226.

54. Ibid., p. 166.

55. Daniel S. Matson and Albert H. Schroeder, eds., "Cordero's Description of the Apache—1796," *New Mexico Historical Review* 32 (Oct., 1957): 335–56.

56. Cortés, *Views from the Apache Frontier*.

57. John, "Views from a Desk in Chihuahua (Merino's Report)," pp. 140–41.

58. Ibid., pp. 146–47. *Establecimientos de paz* for Apaches were peace settlements in Nueva Vizcaya and Sonora near presidios where the natives were provided weekly rations, clothing, and instruction in farming and livestock raising in return for their peaceful relations with Spaniards and services as scouts and auxiliaries on Spanish campaigns against hostile tribes and nations. The policy began with Commandant General Teodoro de Croix in 1779, continued with Jacobo Ugarte y Loyola in 1786–87, and was reestablished in the early 1790s. See Moorhead, *The Presidio*, pp. 245–66.

59. John, "Views from a Desk in Chihuahua (Merino's Report)," p. 148.

60. Ibid., pp. 149–52.

61. Ibid., pp. 152–57.

62. Ibid., p. 154.

63. Ibid., p. 161.

64. Ibid., p. 163.

65. Oakah L. Jones, Jr., "Settlements and Settlers at La Junta de los Rios, 1759–1822," *Journal of Big Bend Studies* 3 (Jan., 1991): 56–57.

66. John, "Views from a Desk in Chihuahua (Merino's Report)," pp. 164–74.

67. Robert S. Weddle, *Spanish Sea: The Gulf of Mexico in North American Discovery, 1500-1685* (College Station: Texas A&M University Press, 1985), pp. 132–33, citing the report of Francisco de Garay.

68. Cyclone Covey, trans. and ed., *Cabeza de Vaca's Adventures in the Unknown Interior of America* (New York: Collier Books, 1961), p. 81.

69. Herbert E. Bolton, *Coronado: Knight of Pueblos and Plains* (New York: Whittlesey House, McGraw-Hill Book Co.; and Albuquerque: University of New Mexico Press, 1949), p. 244, citing Pedro de Castañeda's "relación."

70. Ibid., p. 245.

71. George P. Winship, *The Coronado Expedition, 1540–1542* (Washington, D.C.: Smithsonian Institution, 1896; and Chicago: Rio Grande Press, 1964), pp. 232, 280.

72. The sketch of the bison included originally in López de Gómara's *Historia general de México* appears in Winship, *Coronado Expedition*, p. 233.

73. "Relaciones que envió Don Juan de Oñate de algunas jornadas" (manuscript in Lowery Collection, Library of Congress, Washington, D.C.), in Herbert E. Bolton, ed., *Spanish Exploration in the Southwest, 1542–1706* (New York: Barnes and Noble, 1959, reprint of 1908 ed. by Charles Scribner's Sons), p. 228.

74. Ibid., pp. 228–29.

75. Ibid., p. 229.

76. "Autos de la conquista de la Prova de Coahuila" (manuscript in the Archivo de la Secretaria de Gobierno del Estado de Coahuila), Diary of Fernando del Bosque, 1675, in Bolton, *Spanish Exploration in the Southwest*, p. 298.

77. Covey, *Cabeza de Vaca's Adventures*, pp. 56, 61, 62, 63, 71.

78. Pfefferkorn, *Sonora*, pp. 48–49.

79. Ibid., p. 49.

80. Iris H. W. Engstrand, "Mexico's Pioneer Naturalist and the Spanish Enlightenment," *Historian* 53, no. 1 (Autumn, 1990): 17, 21. See also Engstrand, "Pictures from an Expedition," in *The Sciences* (New York: New York Academy of Sciences, n.d.); Engstrand, "The Unopened Gift: Spain's Contributions to Science during the Age of Enlightenment," *Terra* 22, no. 6 (July–Aug., 1984): 12–17; and Iris H. Wilson, "Spanish Scientists in the Pacific Northwest, 1790–1792," in *Reflections of Western Historians*, ed. John A. Carroll (Tucson: University of Arizona Press, 1969), pp. 31–47.

81. Engstrand, *Spanish Scientists*, pp. 58–59; Cutter, *California in 1792*, pp. 65, 74.

82. Marc Simmons, *The Last Conquistador: Juan de Oñate and the Settling of the Far Southwest* (Norman: University of Oklahoma Press, 1991), p. 175.

MARTA WEIGLE

On Coyotes and Crosses: That Which Is Wild and Wooden of the Twentieth-Century Southwest

Geographically Southwest should be where South and West have crossed. Take everything south of Mason and Dixon's line extended to the Pacific and west of the Mississippi, and what do you get? You get the southwestern part of the United States, certainly, but not the Southwest. The Southwest is a crossing of South and West, but in the sense of breeding to produce offspring. It is neither South nor West, but a mestizo partaking of the characteristics of both parents, and like a child, baffling to both.

—Erna Fergusson, *Our Southwest*, 1940

THE ATCHISON, TOPEKA, & SANTA FE RAILWAY and the Fred Harvey Company opened the Alvarado, billed as the finest railroad hotel on earth, at the Albuquerque, New Mexico, station in May, 1902. The depot complex included both the Indian and Mexican Building, with museum, demonstration, and sales rooms; and the Indian Museum (or Collection) Building, with anthropological exhibits and offices of the Fred Harvey Indian Department. It served as a prototype for similar expositions of regional goods and native peoples elsewhere in the Santa Fe–Harvey system, especially at the Grand Canyon. Some sixty years later, Lawrence Clark Powell called Albuquerque "the heart of hearts, the *cor cordium* . . . that ancient crossing on the Rio Grande," where he stood to survey the Southwest. "I will be even more precise and say just where it would be in Albuquerque: on the station platform of the Alvarado, one of the last of the Harvey Houses and the most beautiful of them all, old gray stucco with turquoise trim, its cool courts and shady patios inviting siesta, its Indian Museum packed with old Pueblo artifacts, its slow heartbeat the coming and going of the Santa Fe trains."[1]

Nearly ninety years after the Alvarado's opening, and some twenty-two after it was razed, Euro Disney opened on Sunday, April 12, 1992, at

Marne-la-Vallée, twenty miles east of Paris. According to *Time* magazine's Richard Corliss, the $4.4 billion, five-thousand-acre theme park and resort inaugurated attractions that "celebrate America the bland and beautiful, and reinvent it, Disney-style; hence the transcontinental, cross-cultural ruckus." Its iconography announced "a complete, hermetic world, an American world that Disney reflects and helped create." The Southwest is part of that world, especially at the Hotel Santa Fe designed by Antoine Predock, whose challenge, as for all Euro Disney designers, was "to be sure that they did not over-intellectualize their work, that it remained . . . what Peter Rummell, the President of the Disney Development Company, has called 'Entertainment Architecture.' "[2]

The corporate Southwest of the transcontinental railroads and international world's fairs drew tourists and art colonists eager to escape the rigors of modern society. From the turn of the century on and especially between the world wars, they glorified and patronized the supposed anachronisms of a place where "the veneer of Americanization . . . runs thin indeed." It was difficult for many "to think of a modern America in a village of the Pueblo Indians, while the inhabitants danced for rain." The imagined Old World, especially Old Spain, also captured them, for "who could dream of the American Way in a mountain hamlet where the sound of the Penitente flute is heard above the thud of the scourges, and Spanish-American villagers perform medieval rites of redemption in Holy Week?"[3] By the 1970s, the antimodern Southwest construct of colorful natives and art colonists had become what John D. Dorst called a postmodern "site"—"a particularly vivid staging of advanced consumer culture . . . an image, an idea, an ideological discourse, an assemblage of texts"—a phenomenon most evident in outsiders' and newcomers' consumption of Santa Fe style and so-called coyote art.[4]

What follows is a look at some twentieth-century images of the "wild" Southwest that are fashioned of wood, usually by men, and represent three periods: first, the railroad's development of the Grand Canyon as a wilderness vantage enhanced by domesticated Hopi Indians and their arts, especially kachina dolls; second, the patronage of art colonists, between world wars, of supposedly anachronistic, Hispanic village culture, especially related to the Penitente Brotherhood, supposed to be from the Middle Ages; and third, the last decade's frenzied proliferation of the howling coyote and other hybrid objects largely dictated by Anglo artists and entrepreneurs of Santa Fe or Southwest style. This selective survey of the woodworked

Southwest draws primary inspiration from Barbara A. Babcock's review of the ceramic Southwest's century of olla maidens in various forms, voluminous literature on pottery, and insatiable market for Indian earthen arts. It is what she called "a long story of the domestication and aestheticization of the Other—a narrative of more than a century of oppression, appropriation, and commodification."[5] In a larger exploration into the twentieth-century development of Southwesternism, the carved Southwest complements the earthenware one.

ENTERTAINMENT ARCHITECTURE: FURNISHING AND FRAMING THE SANTA FE SOUTHWEST

> Silently he stands, gaping at the frightful immensity of the view. . . . The sense of unreality is so strong that one imagines himself standing in the middle of a cyclorama building looking at a painting of highly colored mountains and mysterious gorges, so wonderfully done as to suggest an infinity of space. The silence aids in this delusion, and one half expects to go down some steps out into the noise and reality of a street again.
>
> —John T. McCutcheon, *Doing the Grand Canyon*, 1922

> With respect to the Theme Park, Euro Disney has deliberately been based on a certain view of America. But that view is not necessarily an attempt to duplicate parts of the United States, but rather it is an effort to create an atmosphere that Europeans may recognize because of their familiarity with American movies. Just as the Hotel Cheyenne designed by Robert Stern may bring to mind the set of "High Noon," so the design of Big Thunder Mountain in the Theme Park is reminiscent of movie images of Monument Valley or the Grand Canyon.
>
> —Philip Jodidio, in *Euro Disney Resort*, 1992

In 1897 Charles A. Higgins, Santa Fe Railway passenger agent and publicist, lamented that the Grand Canyon, the "sublimest of gorges and Titan of Chasms," had few "adequate facilities . . . for the general sight-seer, and the world's most stupendous panorama was known principally through [scientific] report"[6] (fig. 1). The Santa Fe Railway exhibited an electric diorama of the Grand Canyon in the Agriculture Building at Buffalo's 1901 Pan-American Exposition in order to give "the majority of visitors. . . . a hint that such a thing as the Grand Canyon of Arizona exists." They presumed "that, having seen this wonderful diorama, you will wish to *experience* the real Grand Canyon." The promised permanent hotel and

Fig. 1. Title page from *Titan of Chasms: The Grand Canyon of Arizona* (Chicago: Rand McNally and Co., 1912), a thirty-two-page booklet. Note the Santa Fe's blue-on-white logo, adopted in 1901. It was said by one etiology to represent a circle, symbolizing the wheels of transportation, around a cross, with the triple meaning of the four compass points, the cross carried by Franciscans accompanying the Conquistadores, and the Indians' sun sign.

terminal facilities, however, were not actually realized until 1904, when the Santa Fe commissioned Chicago architect Charles F. Whittlesey to design a large, first-class hotel near the railroad terminus on the south rim.[7]

Newspapers announced that this venture "would combine the architecture of the 'Swiss chateaux' with that of the 'castles of the Rhine' in native boulders, Douglas fir logs and boards." Built at a cost of $250,000, it opened on January 14, 1905, as El Tovar, named in honor of Pedro de Tovar, the Spanish commander who had been sent by Coronado to explore the Hopi villages. As with all Santa Fe accommodations, El Tovar was managed by the Fred Harvey Company, which issued a booklet in 1909 announcing Whittlesey to have "combined in admirable proportions the Swiss châlet and the Norway villa." The "long, low, rambling edifice" provided ample accommodations for two hundred guests within outside roof and walls "stained a weather-beaten color" and an "inside finish [of] mainly peeled slabs, wood in the rough, and tinted plaster, interspersed with huge wooden beams."[8]

El Tovar (fig. 2) was designed and built in the same "log palace" architectural and decorative style used by Chicago-trained architect Robert Reamer for the Northern Pacific railroad's rustic Old Faithful Inn, constructed of log and native stone, which opened in the summer of 1904 at Yellowstone National Park. Both reflect what Ann Farrar Hyde calls "new attitudes toward the American landscape" in the late nineteenth century, when "Americans began to look at the wilderness as friendly rather than dangerous and as rural simplicity began to look more attractive than urban complexity . . . [and] rather than avoiding the American wilderness, [they] now sought ways to experience it." These new attitudes materialized in the 1880s, when an "Adirondack style using logs and stones as its main materials, with the major décor elements being peeled logs; unfinished boards; and solid, unadorned furniture" developed in the mountains of upper New York State for camps built as "summer and weekend havens for weary urban tycoons." Class distinctions were not supposed to hold at El Tovar, which the 1909 booklet proclaimed to be "not a Waldorf-Astoria, but more like a big country clubhouse, open to any traveler seeking high-class accommodations." Nevertheless, what Hyde calls its split personality of rustic simplicity and resort elegance caused the Grand Canyon hotel to be compared unfavorably with the Old Faithful Inn "because it had 'less of the genuine atmosphere of the wild about it'"[9] (fig. 3).

Fig. 2. *Top*: El Tovar Hotel taken from the roof of Hopi House. *Bottom*: The board-on-batten, Grand Canyon Santa Fe depot, completed in 1909, with El Tovar visible behind and above on the left. (From *Titan of Chasms*, p. 6.)

The El Tovar booklet of 1909 emphasized that "the furniture is mostly of arts and crafts design, made to order at the best eastern factories; nothing cheap nor tawdry is tolerated." Its public rooms, like those in the Old Faithful Inn, were furnished from the trademark line, Craftsman, manufactured by the Gustav Stickley Company, founded in Syracuse, New York,

Fig. 3. El Tovar's lobby, called the Rendezvous, intended to resemble a hunting lodge. ("Phostint" postcard, undated, Detroit Publishing Co.)

in May, 1898. They were popularized by *The Craftsman* magazine, edited by Stickley between 1901 and 1916, the year after his company was bankrupted. According to him:

> The Craftsman furniture is designed solely for use and comfort and durability, and the beauty that is peculiarly its own arises from the directness with which it meets these requirements. . . . While a massive simplicity is the leading characteristic of the style, each piece is finely proportioned and as carefully finished as the work of the old Colonial cabinet-makers, and is as well-fitted to endure. It is my belief that simple, honest structural forms will prevail with but little modification for just so long as a practical, straightforward people asserts its own individuality sufficiently to demand that its home surroundings shall be practical, straightforward things.[10]

Encountering and enjoying such designs was particularly appropriate for accommodations in the newly regenerative wilderness, since "for Stickley as for other craft revivalists, craftsmanship would provide a means of rehabilitating neurasthenics; it promised not social transformation but therapeutic self-renewal within a corporate structure of degraded work and bureaucratic 'rationality.' "[11] Such benefits at least symbolically accrued to guests in the Santa Fe Southwest.

In 1909 the Harvey management pronounced El Tovar "more than a hotel; it is a little village devoted to the entertainment of travelers." Key to that entertainment was Hopi House, designed by Mary Colter to resemble dwellings at Oraibi, Arizona, and opened on January 1, 1905, several days before El Tovar. The booklet promised: "Go inside and you see how these gentle folk live. The rooms are little and low, like their small-statured occupants. The floors and walls are as cleanly as a Dutch kitchen. The Hopis are making 'piki,' twining the raven black hair of the 'manas' in big side swords, smoking corn-cob pipes, building sacred altars, mending moccasins—doing a hundred un-American things."

Not in fact a dwelling, Hopi House was a prime example of Santa Fe–Harvey "staged authenticity," combining a museum and living ethnological display with commercial sales areas. It served as a nucleus for the Grand Canyon's version of the mini-world's fairs set up by the Santa Fe–Harvey corporations trackside, in stations, and at Harvey Houses across the Southwest. According to Burton Benedict, in such world's fairs native peoples were exhibited as craftspeople, curiosities, trophies, or specimens. They were placed in settings that amounted to "display cases reaching millions of potential customers . . . [and] not only selling goods . . . [but] ideas about the relations between nations, the spread of education, the advancement of science, the form of cities, the nature of domestic life, the place of art in society." These expositions appealed to "a rapidly expanding middle class that was interested not just in making money, but in acquiring a whole culture." The goods, ideas, and peoples so displayed and commodified "did not just cater to middle-class taste, they helped form that taste."[12]

By 1932, when Mary Colter designed a rest station and gift shop at Desert View on the east end of Grand Canyon's south rim, that taste for Indians and their goods was changing in emphasis from the ethnological to the aesthetic.[13] Colter's "re-creation" of a Hopi watchtower derived from her archaeological fieldwork, which she documented in 1933 in an eighty-page manual for guides and drivers.[14] The structure's interior, however, was decorated with a variety of prehistoric and contemporary Indian art, while other items were on sale there.

Hopi Watchtower's ground-floor room was patterned after prehistoric great kivas of giant timbers, though in this case using ceiling logs "salvaged from the old Grand View Hotel,—the first hotel ever built at Grand Canyon . . . [and] cut by Pete Berry and his associates—old timers all . . . forty-three years ago" (Colter manual, p. 24). Colter notes that the kiva's simulated Indian furnishings proved problematic because the prehistoric Indians had little furniture except small, tree-trunk benches and tree-burl stools. "Of course a chair with back and arms was quite unknown, and in the development of the Kiva furniture from the burls of trees considerable license was required and taken with this idea of the primitive man." There was even an owl stool fashioned by Anglos from a "grotesque" tree root with "copper deposit" eyes, demonstrating what Colter claims to be "the ingenuity of the Indian in seeing accidental resemblances, and putting them to his own use" (Colter manual, pp. 63–64).

Then thirty-year-old Hopi artist Fred Kabotie painted mythic images on the walls of the tower's first-floor Hopi Room and constructed a snake altar with a sandpainting in the center of the floor. Two carved, wooden kachina dolls from among the extensive Harvey collections made by H. R. Voth, a Mennonite missionary-turned-anthropologist, stood atop the sandpainting.[15] Colter's 1933 manual presented the smaller of these figures in terms familiar to contemporary collectors of kachina dolls:

> [It] is very mysterious . . . [and] has never been identified. One and all of the Indians questioned lately still refuse to give it a name, either because they really do not know what it represents,—or, more likely, because there is some taboo about naming it. . . . Of this figure Voth says: "There is perhaps no piece of Hopi religious paraphernalia, no matter how sacred, concerning which I have had greater difficulty to find out what it is and what it stands for than this figurine" (Colter manual, p. 43).

Although they were completely contrived, commercial structures decorated with a conglomerate of religious images, the Watchtower and kiva nevertheless were blessed in an elaborate, ostensibly Hopi ceremony on May 13, 1933, "covered by 620 newspapers from 45 states, broadcast on the radio, and filmed for Paramount news." By one observer's account, "the strange staccato chant of the Keeper of the Kiva . . . occasionally . . . is interrupted by a cry from the leader of the dancers—a coyote cry, falsetto and unearthly."[16]

Both El Tovar and the Hopi Watchtower helped elevate and frame the wild Grand Canyon as a tourist attraction or sight sacralization, in Dean MacCannell's terms. The hotel provided an apparatus for what Alan Wallach called the typical panoramic convention of spectators climbing a tower in the center of a rotunda. Emerging onto a darkened viewing platform, they saw the lighted painting's "horizon-line roughly [at] . . . eye-level, which meant that viewers experienced a sensation of looking down at the scene," and some even felt "dizziness and *Sehkrank*, or 'see-sickness.'" According to Wallach, "in the panorama, the world is presented as a form of totality; nothing seems hidden; the spectator, looking down upon a vast scene from its center, appears to preside over all visibility."[17]

In his 1922 cartoon-illustrated guide, *Doing the Grand Canyon*, John T. McCutcheon instructed tourists about the conventions of panorama: "When the train stops, you climb a flight that leads to the hotel and purposely avoid glancing over in the direction of the Canyon for fear of getting a premature view which would take away the surprise of the supreme moment." That supreme moment came after "you register leisurely so that you may compose yourself" before emerging from the hotel. "El Tovar stands near the rim of the Canyon with a level stretch of a hundred feet lying between it and the very edge. A low parapet marks the edge and a number of benches are ranged along for the silent contemplation of the view. Beyond the wall there is nothing. . . . It is not until the sightseer reaches the edge that the full force of the view strikes him with a shock that makes him gasp." This was also the "parade ground" where hotel guests gathered to view the sunset, "a widely advertised feature of the Grand Canyon," or to "drink in the new emotions that come with each succeeding moment" of the constantly changing chasm.[18]

The Hopi Watchtower was a more consciously contrived viewing apparatus, one which resembled Jeremy Bentham's panopticon, "a circular prison with a tower at its center designed for the constant surveillance of inmates . . . subject to an anonymous authority, 'the eye of power' or 'sovereign gaze,' as Foucault has called it, that emanated from the tower." Tourists mounting such a vantage, "having reached the topmost point in [the] optical hierarchy . . . experienced a sudden access of power, a dizzying sense of having suddenly come into possession of a terrain stretching as far as the eye could see."[19]

The visitors' "possession" of the canyon was aided by black-glass reflectoscopes installed on the observatory roof and at lower viewing windows. In her manual, Mary Colter explained that they were patterned after devices used by Claude Lorrain, a seventeenth-century French landscape painter, "to *condense* and *simplify* the view he was sketching" (Colter manual, p. 64). On the following page, she noted that "another reason why the pictures shown in these reflectoscopes have so much individuality and charm is due to the *framing* of individual views. The general view of the Grand Canyon is so *overpowering* that separating a section of it for a moment making it a *'framed picture'*—brings it better within one's comprehension."

The "framed picture" that enabled better comprehension of the overpowering view is not far from the "moving picture" set that establishes Europeans' recognition of the United States in Euro Disney. New Mexico architect Antoine Predock designed the resort's Hotel Santa Fe to be "cinematographic in a positive sense." In an interview, he observed that "the giant movie screen . . . is visible at great distance. My architecture in this instance deals with silhouette as does the Theme Park. There is a castle, and there are features jutting out against the sky. The Hotel Santa Fe does that in a similar but not consciously related way." Most prominent is Catherine Feff's 11 x 18.5–meter mural showing "Clint Eastwood and a typical western landscape [to] bring to mind the image of the United States created by the movies." According to Fodor's 1993 guide to Euro Disney:

> A giant portrait of Clint Eastwood glowers down from a drive-in-movie-style screen towering above the parking lot that fronts this hotel complex. Eastwood's dour expression is unintentionally appropriate: Beyond said parking lot, you are confronted with architect Antoine Predoc's [*sic*] 42 dull gray and brown concrete prefabs masquerading as pueblos; the giant fake cacti, the 8-meter (25-foot) lump of concrete intended to look like a volcano, and the rusted automobiles here called sculpture create a mood about as cheerful as a post-war Paris suburb. . . . Luckily, the oppressive atmosphere doesn't extend to the guest rooms, and the faux Navajo patterned quilts on the beds and bright, multicolored mirrors on the walls add a warm touch.[20]

The Hotel Santa Fe's lobby sports the requisite kachinas encased in Plexiglass and wooden furniture built in Santa Fe style. Its sarape-draped staff hand out rate brochures that in November, 1992, contained a welcome from General Manager Chris Newbery, explaining how "the Hotel Santa Fe relies on symbolism to suggest actual and mythical phenomena, . . . creating a sense of the historical and contemporary culture of the West. The legends, landform, water, infinite space and artifacts of this environment . . . the true 'Americana' of the West . . . developed not as literal features but as suggestive themes with multiple intents." Near the hotel's lobby and restaurants, a Trail of Legends sign in English, French, German, Italian, and Spanish instructs: "The contest between man and environment is symbolized by the volcano." Another sign, beside the volcano itself, reads: "The dark, aggressive shape of the volcano contrasts with the flat white sand of the desert plains. It symbolizes not only the geological unrest of the region but also the turbulent nature of the untamed west."[21]

In such mythologizing, 1992 Marne-la-Vallée is not far from 1901 Buffalo, and neither is that remote from today's Southwest theme-park wilds at the Grand Canyon, the Santa Fe Plaza, Bloomingdale's, or elsewhere.

FOLK RELIQUARY: PATRONS AND PENITENTES

Taos is the home of the "Penitentes," one of the weirdest religious sects in the new world. This sect has many thousand members, and their "Moradas," small churches with one window, are scattered over the mountainous portion of the state, usually hidden in some out-of-the-way canyon. The Penitente . . . ritual today consists of self-inflicted lashings with whips made of cactus spines.

—*Lure of the Southwest*, 1934

Moradas are found mainly in New Mexico. These community houses once rang with the ceremonial rites of the *Penitentes*. . . . Now they usually exist only as silent reminders of religious fervor. One, currently lived in by a lively family of five, is shown here. Says Lawrence P. Frank Jr., moviemaker and collector of primitive art, "The description was so irresistible, we bought it sight unseen." The Franks have added modern facilities and a children's wing to their 1852 *morada*, but left the main portion virtually intact. The primitive quality of its interior completely suits their superb collection of *santos* and Indian artifacts. . . . Underneath is a pre-Pueblo Indian pit house that gives the Franks archaeology field trips at home.

—Vera D. Hahn, "Lively Living in a Sanctuary," 1970

From September, 1884, through January, 1885, Charles Fletcher Lummis tramped the continent between Ohio and California, forwarding a weekly letter describing his journey to the fledgling *Los Angeles Times*. His "first acquaintance with those astounding fanatics, the Penitentes . . . [whose] astounding barbarities are still practiced by citizens and voters of the United States" came through the Manuel Chaves family of San Mateo, New Mexico. In February, 1888, Lummis returned to the Chaves ranch. There, on March 29 and 30, accompanied by Ireneo Chaves and a "peon," Lummis photographed at gunpoint several Brotherhood rites, including flagellation, crossbearing, and a simulated crucifixion. In his unpublished memoirs, "As I Remember," he boasts that since *Cosmopolitan* published the photographs in 1889, "the pictures of this medieval ceremony have figured in several of my books and the cult of the Penitentes is known the world over."[22]

Medievalism remained a common theme in much writing about the Penitente Brotherhood. During the 1920s poet Alice Corbin and her artist husband William Penhallow Henderson, prominent art colonists who had moved to Santa Fe in 1916, witnessed the Holy Week rites at Abiquiú, New Mexico.[23] At a night procession of crossbearers they felt "the clock of time had mysteriously turned back. This was not the United States or the Twentieth Century, but the heart of the Middle Ages." Describing Old Spain in New Mexico for a Santa Fe Railway Indian Detours publicity booklet in 1928, Corbin emphasized the "medieval atmosphere of the Spanish villages," where "every year during Lent, the Penitente Brotherhood (*Los Hermanos Penitentes*. . .), an unorthodox survival of the Third Order of Saint Francis, make religious pilgrimages and processions, including cross-bearing and flagellation—medieval symbols of atonement brought to this country by the first Spanish settlers and priests, and common at that date throughout Europe"[24] (figs. 4, 5).

In a 1935 article on regionalism in Southwest writing, Kyle Crichton sarcastically observed that "what the literate visitor to New Mexico hastens to do upon his first visit is fashion an article on the Penitentes." He claimed: "I have never read, for example, a sensible piece on the Penitentes. Aside from the information that the practice had been noted in Italy as early as the Fifteenth Century and was still prevalent in outlying districts of New Mexico, I know nothing of its background. More than that, I know nothing about its meaning to the people who practice it." He deplored "writers who have been living in the section for years [yet are] still so greatly influenced by the 'romance' of it that even their most profound utterances have an unreal and fantastic sound . . . [an] insistence on evading thought by considering everything strange as an isolated instance of individuality rather than a part of the pattern of life." He concluded by urging that "New Mexico become less a part of the Southwest and more a part of the world . . . [and] also that the whole theory of regionalism be laid quietly away with the other relics of a period when it was felt that the way to live was to cease living."[25]

Crichton's is a jaundiced view of what Suzanne Forrest calls "the mystique of the village." After 1900 in New Mexico, successive "waves of artist-intellectuals . . . many of them, especially after World War I, reform-minded progressives eager to put their own distinctive stamp upon the state," attempted "to develop the area economically while preserving the 'quaint and picturesque' nature of its native inhabitants," especially Hispanic villagers. By the 1930s these "intellectuals, as they saw mainstream American society breaking apart, apparently rotten to the core, were more

Fig. 4. A simulated crucifixion by the Penitente Brotherhood on Good Friday afternoon, outside the *morada* (chapel meetinghouse) at Abiquiú, New Mexico, 1920s. The Penitente Brother bound to the cross faces a santo of Our Father Jesus held by two brothers. (Illustration by William Penhallow Henderson, for Alice Corbin Henderson, *Brothers of Light: The Penitentes of the Southwest* [New York: Harcourt, Brace and Co., 1937], p. 47.)

convinced than ever that the New Mexican village held the key to America's future."[26]

In her Indian Detours booklet sketch of 1928, Alice Corbin expressed the fly-in-amber view of those "small sunlit villages of flat-roofed adobe houses . . . [and] Old World charm": "The life in these placitas is almost as simple today as it was of necessity in the days of their settlement; the speech is still that of the Conquistadores, preserving many words long since obsolete in Spain; . . . folksongs in the native tongue are sung and composed." Her patronizing attitude resembles native Santa Fe journalist Ruth Laughlin's, who proclaimed in 1931: "Los pobres of New Mexico are the luckiest poor people in America, if not in the world." They "have been conditioned through countless generations to appreciate the dones de Dios—the beneficent gifts of God." Both women viewed the ethnic poor as if they were compensated for their poverty by colorful cultural riches. As Laughlin described enthusiastically: "Instead of an eleventh-story iron fire escape hung

Fig. 5. Crossbearers, a penitent with cactus tied to his back, and a Penitente Brother dragging the death cart approach the Abiquiú *morada* during a nighttime procession, 1920s. (Illustration by William Penhallow Henderson, *Brothers of Light*, p. 33.)

with washing, there are red geraniums blooming on a low blue window sill. There is no nerve-jangling roar of Elevateds—only the distant 'yip-yip' of coyotes rising through the still night or the nearer braying of burros. . . . There are fiestas, bailes, masses to weave a happy, simple pattern of life."[27]

In order to preserve this changeless, "happy, simple" life, it was necessary to revive and selectively emulate or simulate it. From 1926 through the early 1930s, for example, William Penhallow Henderson designed and produced handmade furniture in Santa Fe because, as his wife explained in *House and Garden* magazine:

> Of late years the marked renaissance of adobe architecture in New Mexico has occasioned a need of Spanish type furniture in keeping with this simple and elemental architecture; and, the supply of originals being limited, this need has been met by the creation of modern furniture based on old traditions. The furniture renaissance of New Mexico may be said to begin with the artists of Taos and Santa Fe who, having built their own adobe houses, then proceeded, like the early Spanish pioneers, to build the furniture to go in them.

Gregorio Gabaldón, Henderson's shop foreman, house carpenter, and native of Santa Fe, had not made furniture until his employer taught him how. Alice Corbin noted his crew of Mexican artisans, whom Henderson "set to work on furniture, for which he supplied the designs as well as the necessary instruction in joining and carving, thus initiating them to the mysteries of their own forgotten craft (so far forgotten, indeed, that most of their own houses were furnished from mail-order catalogues)."[28]

When they attended Penitente Brotherhood rites at Abiquiú, the Hendersons were impressed by the "small and large *Santos* . . . curiously real and living, . . . of native craft, the primitive wood sculpture of this country, in which passion and beauty are instinctively chiseled in the crudely painted wooden features." At the end of the Good Friday night *Tinieblas* (Tenebrae) services in the *morada* (chapel-meetinghouse), the *Hermano Mayor* (leader of the *morada* chapter) "raised his hand, and delivered a short address . . . in Spanish, but intended for *los Americanos* present . . . . We were not to think, he said, that they worshiped—pointing to the images on the altar—these *Muñecas*, these dolls, for themselves. They were the images of the Saints in Heaven; and the ceremonies which we had seen tonight and during the past few days were not savage or barbaric, but were deeply religious mysteries which had been handed down to them by their forefathers from France and Spain."[29]

Santos figured in the founding of the Spanish Colonial Arts Society, launched in 1925, formally incorporated in 1929, and actively supported by both Hendersons, Ruth Laughlin, and other Santa Fe art colonists and business people. During the early 1920s, the Hendersons' Camino del Monte Sol neighbors, writer Mary Austin and painter-sculptor-writer Frank Applegate, began to consider the santos in Applegate's collection. According to Austin:

> We rapidly grew interested in all the old and almost dishabilitated arts of New Mexico, touched with a profound regret for their disappearance. In collecting old pieces, Frank had often recourse to native workmen for repairs, and by this means we came to realize that the capacity for handcraft, of a fine and satisfying quality, though overlaid by modern American neglect, had not completely disintegrated. We began to discuss the possibility of reviving it.

Austin claimed that she first used the term *Spanish Colonial* in her own writing and credited E. Dana Johnson, editor of the *Santa Fe New Mexican* newspaper, with popularizing it at her insistence, so that "Spanish Colonial became a recognized subject of interested comment in the Press."[30]

Charles L. Briggs aptly summarizes the early efforts of the Spanish Colonial Arts Society: "Although the group fostered research and the dissemination of information on *Mexicano* folk art, most of their activities were devoted to providing better marketing outlets. They accordingly organized exhibitions and markets, selecting work for display and awarding prizes. Year-round sales were promoted by the establishment of a Spanish Arts Shop in Santa Fe which operated from 1929 to 1933; Leonora F. Curtin sponsored a Native Market from 1934 until 1939." Anglo elites, "by deciding who could participate in markets and exhibitions . . . even determined what was to be defined as 'traditional' *Mexicano* art." What Briggs called the patrons' "object-fetishism"—their failure to comprehend the dynamics of the carvers' complex relationship to craft, community, and culture—meant that their "efforts did not 'encourage' the artists to meet the needs of their communities . . . [but] rather taught [them] profit-oriented marketing strategies and ways of accommodating the newcomers' aesthetic patterns, . . . thus ultimately further[ing] the very process of commercialization and cultural homogenization that they decried."[31]

In the 1920s and 1930s, antimodernist Anglos collecting "Native American and nineteenth-century *Mexicano* art . . . inflated its monetary value to such a degree that ethnics' homes and churches were denuded through sales and thefts." Still, according to William Wroth,

> during this period, in spite of the enthusiasm of the wealthy Anglo patrons in northern New Mexico, Hispanic crafts never "caught on" nationally in the way the Indian crafts did. Interest was fairly well limited to the Southwest and southern California, the areas in which the adobe hacienda revival was taking place. The major interest in Hispanic crafts was as furnishings for these comfortable Southwestern-style adobe homes. These crafts were not, as were the Indian, viewed as valuable art objects in themselves purchased with an eye for speculation.[32]

With the rapid development of new homes and accommodations during the Southwest tourism and real estate boom in the 1980s, the consumption of both Indian and Hispanic arts began to grow apace. In their 1990 sourcebook, *Santa Fe Design*, for example, Elmo Baca and Suzanne Deats noted that "like Pueblo kachina dolls, *santos* are not merely painted wooden figurines [but] . . . objects of veneration and prayer that are created to bless the home," where they can "make a strong visual impact in a room that contains other folk art elements or Spanish colonial furniture." They go on to observe that "Hopi and Zuni kachina dolls are an important element of Santa Fe design. . . . Popular legend claims that kachina dolls are blessed with a spirit that comes out at night to wander about the house. In Santa Fe nothing having to do with spirit is easily dismissed, so this legend makes it seem especially desirable to have a kachina or a collection of kachinas on your mantel or coffee table [or Grand Canyon]." There, kachinas may be crowded, because "both traditional and contemporary images of death are also found on mantels and shelves in Santa Fe homes. These ghastly skeletons were originally intended to remind the faithful that death was always at hand, but people who collect these figures today seem to concentrate on their primitive anatomy and the grim humor of their facial expressions."[33] Like Clint Eastwood dourly overseeing Euro Disney's American West, these appropriated figures crowded into postmodern display themselves constitute the depthlessness of Santa Fe style, where tradition and heritage are asserted yet "displaced by fragmentary surfaces": what John D. Dorst called "depth as consumable imagery, . . . historical authenticity as a commodified surface effect."[34]

FOLKLORIC COUNTERWORLD: A NEW AGE BESTIARY

If chambers of commerce in Western states that strive for tourist money had imagination, they would arrange hearing places for those who would like to hear coyote voices, just as the national parks provide visible bears; and they would both lure and educate tourists by publishing a truth thus finely expressed by H. E. Anthony of the American Museum of Natural History:

"To many who have heard the ecstatic little prairie wolf greet their camp-fire from out of the dusk, or have arisen at break of dawn and heard his frenzied hymn to the sun, a West without the coyote seems colorless and flat."

—J. Frank Dobie, *The Voice of the Coyote,* 1949

In the untamed Southwest, wild mustangs still run the plains and snakes slither across the barren deserts. So no Southwest home is really complete without a wild animal or two.

—Rebecca Carrier, "Roundup," 1992

The front page of the *Santa Fe Reporter* for December 27, 1989–January 2, 1990, announced a retrospective look at "Boom Town: Santa Fe in the '80s" and featured a full-page photograph of the "Beast of the Decade," a large, carved, howling coyote with a bandanna around its neck. On September 14, 1990, a two-ton, fifteen-foot, turquoise-and-pink, bandanna-draped wooden coyote was installed outside the San Rafael Apartments at the corner of Airport and Zepol Roads in Santa Fe. This monumental "santo" was chainsaw-sculpted from ponderosa pine by Ron McDowell, former union crane operator and Colorado native, and purchased from him by apartment manager Roni Peterson. She had to seek a waiver of city sign laws from the Development Review Committee, whom she told, "I'm new to Santa Fe, and the coyote seems to be a symbol of Santa Fe" (fig. 6). The installation was approved following a split vote, and an August 11 editorial in the *Albuquerque Journal North* expressed the following opinion:

> These proliferating coyote figures are predictable, silent beasts which, other than their shape, have little in common with live coyotes. . . . [The latter] probably have more in common with the real, non-glitz, workaday Santa Fe than [t]his slicked-up cousin. . . . Some worry that the howling coyote may become to Santa Fe what the yellow "happy face" symbol once was to California.
>
> Detractors of coyote art find it cloying and inane. They have their own bumper stickers begging "Just Say No to Coyote Art." For them, at least, these mass-produced, animal clichés symbolize the sanitized *nuevo Santa*

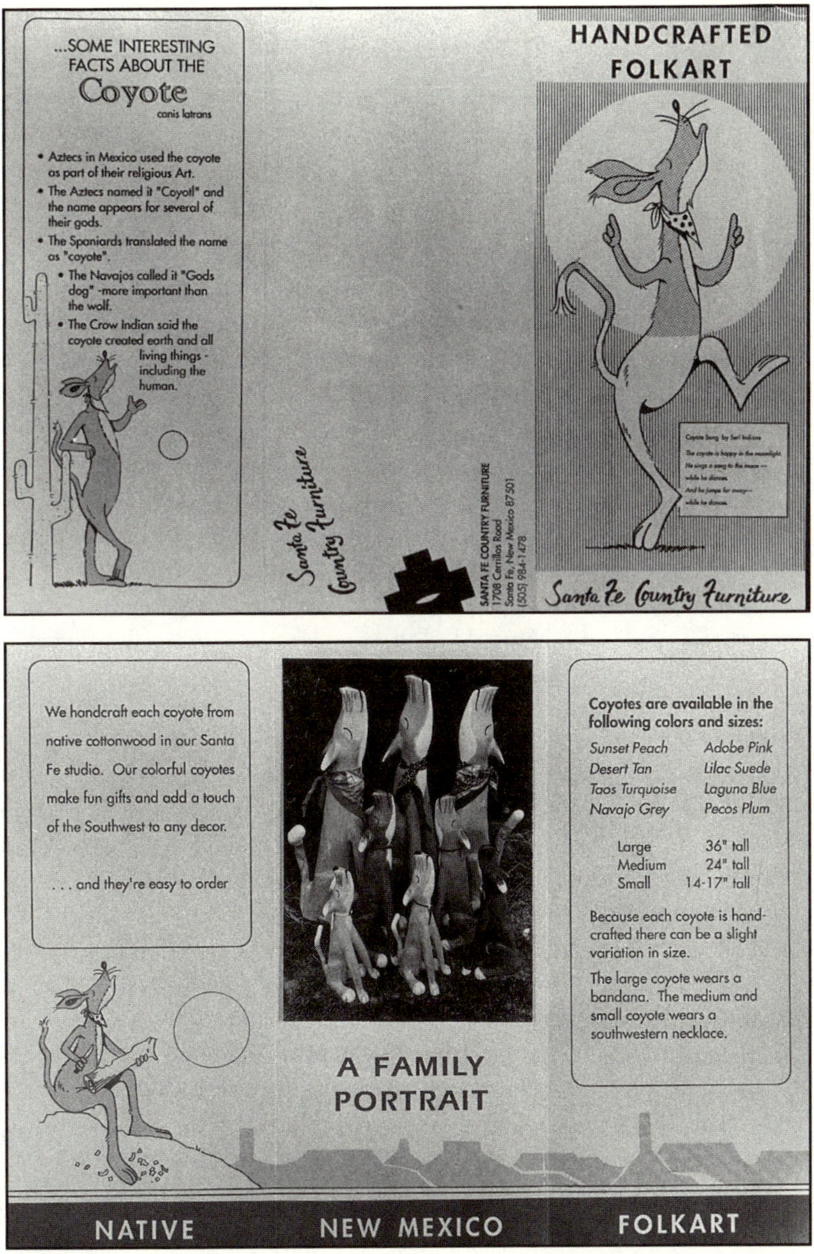

Fig. 6. "Handcrafted Folkart"—three front and three back panels of a late 1980s brochure from Santa Fe Country Furniture (Cerrillos Road, Santa Fe)—reveal that the coyote has been given a mythical heritage and shaped into an icon of the postmodern Southwest.

> *Fe* where the howl of commercialism is beginning to ring louder than long-standing traditions of individualism and fun that doesn't involve money.[35]

In October, 1990, Carmella M. Padilla urged that "the mammoth pastel monster" be replaced by "our own symbol of Santa Fe ... the horned a.k.a. 'horny' toad . . . small, spiny reptile . . . indigenous to the area . . . [that] looks ghastly in pink. What's more, if the horny toad encounters a dangerous foe—a coyote-toting tourist, for instance—it spits blood." Such spittle echoed the satirical lament of Taos columnist Clyde Aragón in August, 1990: "Can we survive the coyote? And just why is it that every single damned one is howling, anyway? How come you never see them scratching or sleeping or putting money into a parking meter? Have you ever *heard* a coyote howl? We're not talking Placido Domingo here. A howling coyote sounds like . . . a cocker spaniel on steroids. And they won't stop once they get started."[36]

Aragón's complaint anticipated the advertising campaign for Coyote Imported Tequila with Natural Wild Herb Flavors. A full-page color ad in the *Albuquerque Journal* on September 7, 1990, showed an apparently real coyote howling on a background butte while three mariachis played at the edge of the brown-sand mesa in the foreground. The framing typography read: " 'Legend has it that they play music to the wild herbs every day before sunset.'. . . Coyote. An experience beyond tequila."

Despite contentions by numerous artists, entrepreneurs, critics, and commentators, howling coyotes and their ubiquitous progeny and paraphernalia are not traceable to Native American, Hispanic, or cowboy folklore and mythology. In this respect they are like the *Wilde-Männle-Tanz*, or dance of the wild men, a tourist attraction in Obertsdorf, Germany. Folklorist Hermann Bausinger has studied this performance, in which fourteen men in "tight linen costumes to which lichen from the mountain forests have been sewn" carry wooden clubs and birch drinking goblets while executing strenuous leaping dances on a stage decorated with fir boughs. It used to be held once every five years, but now happens much more frequently under the influence of tourism. Both scholarly and popular accounts call this an ancient cult custom, but Bausinger showed that, although references to wild people abound and the wild man is known as the "chameleon of the Middle Ages," a thesis of continuity to the present cannot be supported. "Wild people do not originate in cultural expressions of the 'folk' but in predominantly playful customs of the upper social class," he observed, and it is this class that imposes its mythologizing and "playful escape from convention" or counterworld.[37]

The howling wooden coyote and its ilk originate in the playful counterworld and upper social class mythologizing of Davis and Christine Mather and their patronage of Felipe Archuleta, a native New Mexican woodcarver, who died at age eighty on January 1, 1991. In an obituary for the following day's *Santa Fe New Mexican*, Davis Mather, whose successful Folk Art Gallery in Santa Fe features Archuleta's work, was quoted as claiming that "Archuleta is regarded by some art experts as 'the folk artist of the century' in the United States." During the early 1980s, Christine Mather was curator of Spanish Colonial Art at Santa Fe's Museum of International Folk Art, which for several years that decade had a special exhibit of Archuleta's pieces. She reported that Archuleta "never felt comfortable with his designation as an artist, but he enjoyed the recognition his carvings brought him . . . [although] he never traveled to any event featuring his work." Both Mathers said Archuleta has many imitators but they believe "none has captured the raw, ferocious nature of his carved animals."

In September, 1989, Johathan Taylor chronicled "the coyote connection" for the *Los Angeles Daily News*. During the mid-1960s, Archuleta had a religious experience, quit his job as a union carpenter, and "scratched out a living carving coyotes, jaguars, orangutans, pigs and various other creatures and selling them when he could." In the 1970s, Davis Mather, "a native of Princeton, N.J., who moved to Santa Fe as a penniless graduate student . . . with the idea of becoming a free-lance writer," happened to discover Archuleta and wrote an article about him that appeared in several national art magazines. After being asked to help gallery owners acquire Archuleta pieces, Mather "set aside his writing aspirations and began to act as a broker for Archuleta's increasingly popular work."[38] This growing workload led Archuleta to hire assistant Alonzo Jiménez, who is credited with creating the now-infamous howling coyote. In 1977 he also hired David Alvarez, originally from Oakland, California, who later left and began making coyotes with his brothers Max, Elmer, Rory, and Duane.

In their canonical *Santa Fe Style*, which since its 1986 publication has sold some two hundred thousand copies, Christine Mather and Sharon Woods romanticized Felipe Archuleta as "a true original": "For all the fame and recognition he has received as the creator of folk art animals and as master for a group of followers, Archuleta stubbornly refuses to be bought out or in, to change his lifestyle, be gracious, or even friendly—or to compromise an art that seems to spring full-blown from a mysterious source in his psyche." They cited "followers Alonzo Jiménez, David Alvarez, and Felipe's son Leroy [who] have developed personal styles using the same media, technique, and compositions originated by Felipe Archuleta."[39]

The photograph on page 121 of *Santa Fe Style* shows six painted coyotes on or beside a white pedestal in front of a white wall hung with eleven snakes. The caption reads: "Carved and painted wooden snakes by Paul Lutonsky and coyotes howling at the moon by Alonzo Jiménez have captured the imaginations of Santa Fe residents and visitors. The snakes dangle over doors and windows, replace a framed picture over the living-room couch, and slither across *bancos*." Johathan Taylor quoted Davis Mather:

> "People call me and say, 'I'm in New Canaan (Conn.), and I've got *Santa Fe Style* (a bible of Southwestern design . . .) in my hand,' " the intense, fast-talking Mather said, with a sense of wonderment in his voice. " 'I'm looking at page 121: can you sell me an Alonzo Jiménez coyote?' "

Taylor concluded his coyote "mythology" with a visit to interview David and Duane Alvarez in their workshop on the outskirts of Santa Fe. "Not quite the artistic innovators that the now-retired Archuleta or Jiménez were, the Alvarezes have nonetheless established a reputation as among the finest animal carvers in the state, with their work selling around the country. . . . Those wildly colored, purposely primitive animals are not exactly art (though this is debatable), not really mass production. But they are popular. Or, as David Alvarez said, 'I can make them lifelike, but folk art sells.' " Alvarez's remarks fit the contemporary definition of folk art proposed by Elmo Baca and Suzanne Deats in *Santa Fe Design*. "In Santa Fe today, it seems . . . appropriate to use the term *folk art* to describe intentionally unrefined decorative objects, such as Felipe Archuleta's animal sculptures, Paul Lutonsky's brightly colored snakes, and Alonzo Jiménez's howling coyotes. Brilliant color and good humor are often components of folk art made in Santa Fe or imported to Santa Fe from Mexico. These objects add a charming touch to rooms that otherwise might seem to take themselves too seriously."[40]

Colorful folk art from south of the border accents a house belonging to Stanley Marcus, "the legendary force behind the phenomenal growth and influence of Dallas's Neiman-Marcus, [who] is generally regarded as one of our culture's leading authorities on taste," at least according to

Stephen Parks, who interviewed him in 1988. Parks found Marcus's

> summer home just outside Santa Fe . . . instructive of who the man is, what he loves, and how he treats the things he loves. From the outside, the house looks small, square, plain, and so it is. . . . It is a house designed for viewing, but eminently livable. . . . Nothing inside the house is showy, everything is quiet—or quietly displayed—and exquisite, including a remarkable collection of Mimbres pots, some stunning Navajo Chief blankets and Plains Indian beadwork. For counterpoint, Marcus and his wife, Linda, collect bright and vibrant pieces of Mexican folk art.[41]

The Marcuses' counterworld "counterpoint" of Native American and Mexican collectibles on tasteful view recalls El Tovar's Rendezvous lobby of dark-stained logs furnished, as described in the 1909 booklet, with "gray Navajo rugs. . . , cosy tête-a-têtes and easy chairs, . . . heads of deer, elk, moose, mountain sheep, and buffalo, mingling with curiously shaped and gaudily tinted Indian jars from the Southwest pueblos, [and] an old-fashioned clock."[42]

INCISED SOUTHWESTERNISM

> To believe that the Orient was created—or, as I call it, "Orientalized"—and to believe that such things happen simply as a necessity of the imagination, is to be disingenuous. The relationship between Occident and Orient is a relationship of power, of domination, of varying degrees of a complex hegemony, and is quite accurately indicated in the title of K. M. Panikkar's classic *Asia and Western Dominance*. The Orient was Orientalized not only because it was discovered to be "Oriental" in all those ways considered commonplace by an average nineteenth-century European, but also because it *could be*—that is, submitted to being—*made* Oriental.
>
> —Edward W. Said, *Orientalism*, 1978

In her study of "New Mexican Rebecca" olla maidens, Barbara A. Babcock declared that "the Southwest *is* America's Orient." She cited Edward W. Said while claiming: "Like the Orient, the Southwest is an idea that has 'a history and a tradition of thought, imagery, and vocabulary that have given it reality and presence in and for' the rest of America." The feminized, domesticated, and aestheticized Other represented by the Native American woman potter and her wares is central to this "thought, imagery, and vocabulary."[43] Not so central to the trope, at least until the last twenty or so years, is the representation of any woodworker or woodworked arts tradition.

Babcock asked, "Why has a traditionally dressed woman shaping or carrying an *olla*, a water jar, become *the* classic metonymic misrepresentation of the Pueblo, and why has Anglo America invested so much in this image for more than a century?" One answer is that the female, ceramic Southwest is safer than the male, woodworked one, and the pot-shaping or pot-bearing woman easier to appropriate and dominate than the knife-wielding man. As Babcock noted, "This authorized image of the 'civilized,' domestic, and feminized Pueblo was popularized at the very moment when 'wild' nomadic [and masculinized] Apaches were still killing white people and eluding General Crook in the same southwestern spaces." After visiting the Santa Fe–Harvey Indian and Mexican Building on the Albuquerque station platform in 1903, a tourist wrote: "Those of us who had previously resisted the Indian bacilli here became inoculated, and we are all now hunting for blankets, baskets, and the gory scalping-knife."[44] Woodwork and pottery have somewhat distinctive histories as emblems of an emerging Santa Fe style. Although kachina dolls were collected almost as long as pottery and became especially popular items soon after 1900, their carvers—unlike potters—generally were not pictured either at work or with their crafted products in tourist and art colonist literature and productions.[45]

In large part because it is European, Catholic, and folk instead of indigenous and primitive, the Hispanic Southwest has been more slowly assimilated into Southwesternism than have Indian cultures. But it is perhaps perceived as no less dangerous, at least with respect to the Penitente Brotherhood. Charles F. Lummis claimed to have been shot at by Brothers angry over his 1880s disclosures, and the legend motif of the grim dangers associated with documenting Brotherhood rites can thus be traced to him. To this day it remains a cherished belief-legend that received fresh impetus when Carl N. Taylor, free-lance writer and University of New Mexico instructor, was murdered at Cedar Crest in the Sandia Mountains on February 5, 1936. Because Taylor had just completed an article on the Brotherhood for *Today Magazine*, its editor and his literary agent suggested that "Taylor may have been the victim of some strange Penitente plot." Although Modesto Trujillo confessed to the killing while robbing Taylor and the district attorney's investigations absolved the Brotherhood entirely, scores of newspapers printed erroneous versions under lurid titles, and a so-called documentary, "The Penitente Murder Case," was filmed in Hollywood and banned in New Mexico by Governor Clyde Tingley.[46]

This unfortunate furor likely influenced Mabel DeLaMater Scacheri's egregious account, titled "The Penitentes: Murderous or Misguided?" She described the guard who objected to her husband Mario's attempts to photograph a Brotherhood ritual as "a man with the wild, staring gaze of a marijuana smoker," explaining to her *Family Circle* readers in 1936 that "marijuana is a narcotic plant which makes men mad, and in Penitente country it is best not to defy it." Scacheri probably also confused the Taylor murder accounts with sensationalized views of gangs of *grifos*, or marijuana smokers and peddlers, in El Paso, Texas, in the early 1930s.[47]

By the time the "stubbornly" idiographic, ungracious, and unfriendly Felipe Archuleta was successfully selling his carved, "raw, ferocious" animals in the late 1970s and 1980s, contemporary Hispanic wood-carvers were gaining local and national attention as fine folk artists. The Spanish Colonial Arts Society had revived the Native Spanish Market in 1965, and from 1967 to 1971 it was organized in conjunction with the Indian Market. Since 1972 a separate and growing Spanish Market has been held annually on the Santa Fe Plaza during the last weekend of July, and many of its artists garner handsome profits for "fine art" pieces. In 1992, for example, Charles M. Carrillo, an Abiquiú Penitente brother, advertised himself as an "award winning santero" doing "museum quality traditional santos made with home-made pigments, cottonwood root and hand-adzed panels."[48]

The late 1980s marked the region's final containment within the Southwesternism paradigm. According to George Kubler: "The triumph of one culture over another is usually marked by the virtual cessation of the art of the vanquished, and its replacement by the art of the conqueror. When the offending objects and monuments finally cease to correspond to any living behavior, they become symbolically inert. They then are 'safe' to play with in recombinations emptied of previous vital meanings, as in tourist souvenirs, antiquarian reconstructions, or archaizing revivals."[49] Both the chainsaw art massacre and the growing market for handcrafted furniture attest to the symbolic inertness of "safe," mostly male, largely Mexican or Indian woodworked art forms.

Santa Fe cowboy furniture maker L. D. Burke III perhaps best exemplifies this "crossing" or commerce in comic, counterworld conquest. In Suzanne Deats and John Villani's *Interior Furnishings Southwest: The Sourcebook of the Best Production Craftspeople*, Burke is presented as doing what the *New York Times* called "some of the most adventurous work coming out of the Great Southwest today," primarily "original and one-of-a-kind furniture, hand adzed, painted, and waxed for 'a finish that feels like a newborn calf.'"

> "As an artist, I'm working the fine line between cornpone and slick stuff," he admits cheerfully. His idiosyncratic furniture, ruggedly built to last for three generations, is frequently emblazoned with original cowboy sayings, sometimes picked out in brass nail heads: "Ya can tell a winner by the way he plays a losin' hand," and "If you take life seriously, how do you explain yesterday?"
>
> Burke's furniture is also embellished with a variety of artifacts including horseshoes, spurs, horns, silver dollars, and other Western paraphernalia. The overall look is unabashedly romantic, recalling the bygone glories of range life and the Code of the West. L. D. Burke's furniture brings it back alive.[50]

Burke, who came to Santa Fe from Boston in 1983, opened the Pink Church at 1516 Pacheco Street in June, 1991. When interviewed by reporter Jan Best for *The Santa Fe New Mexican*, Burke claimed of his structure—painted pink and purple and designed in a Hispanic territorial mission style—which serves as his workshop and gallery:

> "I really didn't design the church. . . . The church designed itself. I did nothing but carry it out. I consider church architecture the most beautiful architecture in New Mexico. . . ."
>
> Burke holds to no particular sect himself but has been a Course in Miracles student for many years. . . . "This is Santa Fe, so I can say I've had lots of past lives as a cleric and a monk. . . . This room, this environment, makes me feel at home."

In his simulated sanctuary, L. D. Burke is a latter-day William Penhallow Henderson who employs four carpenters from El Salvador: Melquisedec Acevedo, Will Martínez, and brothers Fabian and Daniel Arias. Despite its location in an industrial-commercial area,

> "What's amazing is the hunger that's out there for this sort of building," Burke said. "A day doesn't pass but four or eight people drop in, walking around and looking at it.
>
> "This is not some tongue-in-cheek parody of a church. This is an honest building that demanded to be built. That's the way with all work I do—I just sort of implement it."[51]

Finally, perhaps, there are two victims of Santa Fe style: the one made famous by artist Jerome Milord's postcard-turned-poster in 1989 and the one "drawn and quartered" by cartoonist Jon Richards in the *Santa Fe Reporter* of December 11–17, 1991. Milord's poster portrays a woman in the full Santa Fe style regalia of boots, prairie skirt, Navajo blouse, concho belt, squash-blossom necklace, bracelets, and rings who lies with eyes closed, face up on the floor beneath the viga ceiling of her living room. A carved, Spanish colonial *trastero* stands in the corner, and a pink, howling coyote sits in front of the banco beside the kiva fireplace. Six carved snakes decorate the wall above the banco, while a seventh is partly visible slithering out the door just beyond the woman's head.[52] Richards's cartoon, also entitled "Another Victim of Santa Fe Style," simply shows a pickup truck, loaded with cut logs and sporting a tail-gate sign reading "Piñon Firewood," leaving a hill of stumps.

Santa Fe style became its own victim on December 24, 1992, when Ann Japenga announced in the *Los Angeles Times* that the nation was "On a Northwest Course": "Forget adobes and coyotes and deserts. Southwest style has come and gone. Think cabins and salmon and forests, as the anti-style of Seattle takes over what we see, hear and wear." Someone, however, forgot to tell actress Shirley MacLaine, interviewed by Bob Thomas for an Associated Press release printed in the *Albuquerque Journal* of January 26, 1993:

> Q. Are you still living in the state of Washington?
>
> A. Yes, but I'm going to sell the place and move to New Mexico. I'm interested in the high desert now. There are too many Californians now in Washington. . . .
>
> Q. What do you do out there in New Mexico?
>
> A. First of all, I have a satellite (dish), so I have all the shows I have to see. "Entertainment Tonight," "Nightline" and so forth. I write, I read, I've got friends there, I'm learning how to dowse for water, I'm learning what the crystal deposits are in the mountains and the high desert lands. I'm learning about the plants and the birds and Native American stuff.

In this inversion Shirley MacLaine brings to a close nearly a century of Southwesternism. Her New Age "wilds" combine the cinematographic, wild Old West of Clint Eastwood and L. D. Burke III with the postmodern New Southwest. This Southwest has been wildly inscribed on panoramic surfaces at the Grand Canyon and elsewhere in the tamed wilderness and in staged dwellings from El Tovar and Hopi House to Euro Disney's Hotel Santa Fe.

NOTES

I would here like to express my gratitude to the members of the Department of History at the University of Texas at Arlington, especially Stephen Maizlish, chair of the Webb Lectures Committee, and Richard Francaviglia, director of the Center for Greater Southwestern Studies and the History of Cartography, for giving me the opportunity to develop this paper and for their hospitality during the lectures.

Chapter epigraph is from Erna Fergusson, *Our Southwest* (New York: Alfred A. Knopf, 1940), pp. 3–4.

1. Lawrence Clark Powell, *Southwestern Book Trails: A Reader's Guide to the Heartlands of New Mexico and Arizona* (Albuquerque: Horn and Wallace, 1963), p. 2. On the Albuquerque station complex, see Marta Weigle, "Exposition and Mediation: Mary Colter, Erna Fergusson, and the Santa Fe/Harvey Popularization of the Native Southwest, 1902–1940," *Frontiers: A Journal of Women's Studies* 12, no. 3 (1992): 117–18, 122–25.

2. Richard Corliss, "Voilà! Disney Invades Europe. Will the French Resist?" *Time* magazine, Apr. 20, 1992, pp. 82, 84; Philip Jodidio, "Introduction," in *Euro Disney Resort*, English edition of a special issue of *Connaissance des arts* (Paris: Société de Promotion Artistique, 1992), p. 6.

3. Workers of the Writers' Program of the Works Projects Administration in the State of New Mexico, comps., *New Mexico: A Guide to the Colorful State*, American Guide Series (New York: Hastings House, 1940), p. 3.

4. John D. Dorst, *The Written Suburb: An American Site, an Ethnographic Dilemma* (Philadelphia: University of Pennsylvania Press, 1989), p. 3. On the development of Santa Fe style and the postmodern Southwest, see Marta Weigle, "Southwest Lures: Innocents Detoured, Incensed Determined," *Journal of the Southwest* 32 (1990): 499–540.

5. Barbara A. Babcock, " 'A New Mexican Rebecca': Imaging Pueblo Women," *Journal of the Southwest* 32 (1990): 400. I am deeply indebted to Barbara Babcock for important insights and lively dialogue on these matters of Southwesternism.

6. C. A. Higgins, "The Titan of Chasms," in *The Grand Canyon of Arizona: Being a Book of Words from Many Pens, about the Grand Canyon of the Colorado River in Arizona*, published by the Passenger Department of the Santa Fe (Chicago: Poole Bros., 1906), p. 11. For more on the Santa Fe's advertising campaigns to bolster corporate image and earnings following its 1896 financial reorganization, see Sandra d'Emilio and Suzan Campbell, *Visions and Visionaries: The Art and Artists of the Santa Fe Railway* (Salt Lake City, Utah: Peregrine Smith Books, 1991). Epigraphs for this section are from John T. McCutcheon, *Doing the Grand Canyon*, illustrated with cartoons by the author (Fred Harvey Co., 1922), p. 5; and Jodidio, "Introduction," *Euro Disney Resort*, pp. 7, 9.

7. "The Grand Canyon of Arizona: Over a Mile Deep / Thirteen Miles Wide / Two Hundred and Seventeen Miles Long," published by AT & SF Railway General Passenger Office (Chicago: Rogers and Smith Co., Aug. 10, 1901).

8. J. Donald Hughes, *In the House of Stone and Light: A Human History of the Grand Canyon* (Arizona: Grand Canyon Natural History Assoc., 1978), pp. 68, 70. The 1909 booklet is entitled *Hotel El Tovar on the Rim of the Grand Canyon, Management of Fred Harvey* and was copyrighted by Santa Fe Railway traffic manager W. J. Black. It is unpaginated, and all subsequent references come from *Hotel El Tovar: Historical Review, Grand Canyon of Arizona*, a 1977 reprint with a new cover, published by Fred Harvey, Inc.

9. Ann Farrar Hyde, *An American Vision: Far Western Landscape and National Culture, 1820–1920* (New York: New York University Press, 1990), pp. 258–59, 274.

10. Robert Judson Clark, ed., *The Arts and Crafts Movement in America, 1876–1916*

(Princeton, N.J.: Art Museum, Princeton University, 1972), pp. 9, 10. Stickley's discussion of his post-1900 abandonment of "standard patterns and finishes" is from his 1906 *Chips from the Craftsman Workshops*, as reprinted in Stephen Gray and Robert Edwards, eds., *Collected Works of Gustav Stickley* (New York: Turn of the Century Editions, 1981), p. 19. I am grateful to Laura Wilson for the latter reference.

11. T. J. Jackson Lears, *No Place of Grace: Antimodernism and the Transformation of American Culture, 1880–1920* (New York: Pantheon Books, 1981), p. 69.

12. Burton Benedict, "The Anthropology of World's Fairs," in Benedict et al., *The Anthropology of World's Fairs: San Francisco's Panama Pacific International Exposition of 1915* (London and Berkeley: Lowie Museum of Anthropology with Scolar Press, 1983), pp. 2, 43–45. On Hopi House, see Marta Weigle, "From Desert to Disney World: The Santa Fe Railway and the Fred Harvey Company Display the Indian Southwest," *Journal of Anthropological Research* 45 (1989): 120–26; and Weigle, "Exposition and Mediation," pp. 125–27.

13. The Exposition of Indian Tribal Arts, which opened at Manhattan's Grand Central Art Galleries in 1931, was billed as the first exhibition of "Indian art as art, *not* ethnology," and according to Molly H. Mullin, "reflected elite responses to the rise of consumer capitalism" whereby "newly imagined [American] identities celebrated cultural pluralism, particularly as expressed through commodities validated as art" ("The Patronage of Difference: Making Indian Art 'Art, Not Ethnology,' " *Cultural Anthropology* 7 [1992]: 395).

14. Mary Colter's mimeographed "*Manual* for Drivers and Guides—Descriptive—of *The Indian Watchtower* at Desert View and Its Relation, Architecturally, to *The Prehistoric Ruins of the Southwest*" (Grand Canyon National Park, Ariz.: Fred Harvey Co., 1933) is in the University of Arizona Library Special Collections.

15. On Henry R. Voth and his Harvey Company collecting, see Barton Wright, *Hopi Material Culture: Artifacts Gathered by H. R. Voth in the Fred Harvey Collection* (Flagstaff, Ariz.: Northland Press and Heard Museum, 1979), especially "H. R. Voth, Ethnologist," by Fred Eggan, pp. 1–7.

16. Virginia L. Grattan, *Mary Colter: Builder upon the Red Earth* (Flagstaff, Ariz.: Northland Press, 1980), p. 80.

17. Dean MacCannell, *The Tourist: A New Theory of the Leisure Class*, rev. ed. (1976; New York: Schocken Books, 1989), pp. 44–45; Alan Wallach, "Making a Picture of the View from Mount Holyoke," *Bulletin of the Detroit Institute of Arts* 66, no.1 (Nov. 1, 1990): 37, 38. I am grateful to James Moore, director of the Albuquerque Museum, for the latter reference.

18. McCutcheon, *Doing the Grand Canyon*, pp. 3, 5, 15, 17.

19. Wallach, "Making a Picture," pp. 37–38.

20. Predock in *Connaissance des arts* interview, *Euro Disney Resorts*, pp. 49, 70; *Fodor's Euro Disney: The Complete Guide to Disney's Newest Park, and the Best of Paris* (New York: Fodor's Travel Pub., 1993), p. 69.

21. Both the brochure and the sign texts were secured during my brief, late-afternoon visit to the Hotel Santa Fe on November 26, 1992. The four "trails" from the lobby-dining area to the "pueblo" room blocks are the Trail of Artifacts (snake emblem), Trail of Water (trout emblem), Trail of Monuments (roadrunner emblem), and Trail of Legends (buffalo emblem).

22. Turbesé Lummis Fisk and Keith Lummis, *Charles F. Lummis: The Man and His West* (Norman: University of Oklahoma Press, 1975), pp. 44–45. See also Marc Simmons, *Two Southwesterners: Charles Lummis and Amado Chaves* (Cerrillos, N.Mex.: San Marcos Press, 1968); and Michael Heisley, "Lummis and Mexican-American Folklore," in *Chas. F. Lummis: The Centennial Exhibition Commemorating His Tramp Across the Continent*, ed. Daniela P. Moneta (Los Angeles: Southwest Museum, 1985), pp. 60–67. References to Lum-

mis's Penitente publications are in Marta Weigle, comp., *A Penitente Bibliography* (Albuquerque: University of New Mexico Press, 1976), pp. 94–95. The inaccurate assertions about the Penitentes in the epigraph for this section are from *Lure of the Southwest: History, Legend, Romance*, published by Mobilgas (Dallas, Tex.: Magnolia Petroleum Co., 1934), p. 8. For an overview of the history and rituals of the Penitente Brotherhood, see Marta Weigle, *Brothers of Light, Brothers of Blood: The Penitentes of the Southwest* (1976; reprint ed., Santa Fe: Ancient City Press, 1989). The second epigraph is from Vera D. Hahn, "Lively Living in a Sanctuary," *American Home*, March, 1970, p. 56. According to the jacket copy of Larry Frank's seventy-five-dollar *New Kingdom of the Saints: Religious Art of New Mexico, 1780–1907* (Santa Fe: Red Crane Books, 1992), Frank "studied medieval art in Paris and . . . during travels to many Romanesque and Gothic churches in England, France, Italy, and Spain." Back in the United States, "he found that the counterpart which continued the tradition for him was the linear and stylized design of the *santos* [and] he has been a collector of *santos* for thirty-five years."

23. On the Taos and Santa Fe art colonies see, for example, Van Deren Coke, *Taos and Santa Fe: The Artist's Environment, 1882–1942* (Albuquerque: University of New Mexico Press, 1963); Kay Aiken Reeve, *Santa Fe and Taos, 1898–1942: An American Cultural Center* (El Paso: Texas Western Press, 1982); Marta Weigle and Kyle Fiore, *Santa Fe and Taos: The Writer's Era, 1916–1941* (Santa Fe: Ancient City Press, 1982); and Arrell Morgan Gibson, *The Santa Fe and Taos Art Colonies: Age of the Muses, 1900–1942* (Norman: University of Oklahoma Press, 1983). An important study of the Taos art colony is by Sylvia Rodríguez, "Art, Tourism, and Race Relations in Taos: Toward a Sociology of the Art Colony," *Journal of Anthropological Research* 45 (1989): 77–99.

24. Alice Corbin Henderson, *Brothers of Light: The Penitentes of the Southwest*, with illustrations by William Penhallow Henderson (New York: Harcourt, Brace and Co., 1937), p. 37; Henderson, "Old Spain in New Mexico," in *They Know New Mexico: Intimate Sketches by Western Writers*, issued by the Passenger Department, Atchison, Topeka, and Santa Fe Railway (Chicago: Rand McNally and Co., 1928), pp. 13–14.

25. Kyle Crichton, "Cease Not Living," *New Mexico Quarterly* 5 (1935): 74, 75, 76. See also Marta Weigle, "The Penitente Brotherhood in Southwestern Fiction: Notes on Folklife and Literature," in *The American Self: Myth, Ideology, and Popular Culture*, ed. Sam B. Girgus (Albuquerque: University of New Mexico Press, 1981), pp. 221–30.

26. Suzanne Forrest, *The Preservation of the Village: New Mexico's Hispanics and the New Deal* (Albuquerque: University of New Mexico Press, 1989), pp. 47–48, 62.

27. Henderson, "Old Spain in New Mexico," pp. 13-14; Ruth Laughlin, *Cabelleros* (1931; rev. ed., Caldwell, Idaho: Caxton Printers, 1945), pp. 300, 301.

28. Alice Corbin, "Furniture for Spanish Colonial Homes," *House and Garden*, July, 1928, pp. 62, 92, 106, as cited in Lonn Taylor and Dessa Bokides, *New Mexican Furniture, 1600–1940: The Origins, Survival, and Revival of Furniture Making in the Hispanic Southwest* (Santa Fe: Museum of New Mexico Press, 1987), p. 219.

29. Henderson, *Brothers of Light*, p. 55.

30. Mary Austin, "Frank Applegate," *New Mexico Quarterly* 2 (1932): 214. See also Marta Weigle, "The First Twenty-five Years of the Spanish Colonial Arts Society," in *Hispanic Arts and Ethnohistory in the Southwest: New Papers Inspired by the Work of E. Boyd*, ed. Marta Weigle with Claudia Larcombe and Samuel Larcombe (Albuquerque: University of New Mexico Press; Santa Fe: Ancient City Press, 1983), pp. 181–203.

31. Charles L. Briggs, "The Role of *Mexicano* Artists and the Anglo Elite in the Emergence of a Contemporary Folk Art," in *Folk Art and Art Worlds*, ed. John Michael Vlach and Simon J. Bronner, with a new introduction (1986; Logan: Utah State University Press, 1992),

pp. 207–208, 217, 218. Sarah Deutsch sees a similar dilemma in the New Deal cultural revival programs: "By channeling relief funds for Hispanic areas into such projects as Spanish colonial crafts training, governmental programs encouraged cultural isolation, whether or not they intended it. Anti-modernist Anglos, grappling with real problems of geographic isolation and poverty in the villages, saw in colonial cultural revival the economic salvation of the Hispanic villages, and the spiritual salvation of modern America. But however beneficent their impulse, they often did not understand Hispanic villagers' mores and desires, and their movement had other implications" (*No Separate Refuge: Culture, Class, and Gender on an Anglo-Hispanic Frontier in the American Southwest, 1880–1940* [New York: Oxford University Press, 1987], p. 208).

32. Briggs, "Anglo Elite," p. 217; William Wroth, "Introduction: Hispanic Southwestern Craft Traditions in the 20th Century," in *Hispanic Crafts of the Southwest*, ed. William Wroth (Colorado Springs: Taylor Museum of the Colorado Springs Fine Arts Center, 1977), p. 6. On the construction of Hispanic Southern California, 1850-1920, see Kevin Starr, *Inventing the Dream: California through the Progressive Era* (New York: Oxford University Press, 1985), esp. pp. 3–127.

33. Elmo Baca and Suzanne Deats, *Santa Fe Design* (Lincolnwood, Ill.: Publications International, 1990), pp. 210, 232. See also Elmo Baca with Elaine Markoutsas, *Southwest Expressions* (Lincolnwood, Ill.: Publications International, 1992), esp. pp. 31–32, 169. On death figures, see Marta Weigle, "Ghostly Flagellants and Doña Sebastiana: Two Legends of the Penitente Brotherhood," *Western Folklore* 36 (1977): 135–47.

34. Dorst, *Written Suburb*, p. 108.

35. Jim Danneskiold, "Panel OKs Howling Coyote Art: 15-Foot Sculpture Will Greet Apartment Dwellers," *Albuquerque Journal North*, Aug. 3, 1990, p. 1; editorial, "Santa Fe Style?" *Albuquerque Journal North*, Aug. 11, 1990, p. 4. This section's epigraphs are from J. Frank Dobie, *The Voice of the Coyote* (Boston: Little, Brown, 1949), p. xvi, and Rebecca Carrier, field editor, "Roundup," *Southwest Sampler*, Spring, 1992, p. 14. See also Theresa Meléndez, "The Coyote," in *American Wildlife in Symbol and Story*, ed. Angus K. Gillespie and Jay Mechling (Knoxville: University of Tennessee Press, 1987), pp. 203–33.

36. Carmella M. Padilla, "Enough Coyotes, Already," *Santa Fe Reporter*, Oct. 10–16, 1990, p. 5; Clyde Aragón, "Can We Survive the Coyote?" *Taos News*, Aug. 9, 1990, B-10.

37. Hermann Bausinger, *Folk Culture in a World of Technology*, trans. Elke Dettmer (1961, 1971; trans., Bloomington: Indiana University Press, 1990), pp. 140, 143.

38. Johathan Taylor, "The Coyote Connection," *Los Angeles Daily News*, as reprinted in *Santa Fe New Mexican*, Sept. 24, 1989, C-1. Next to this reprint, which begins by speculating that "maybe Indian mythology is right about the coyote . . . [being] God's Dog," is an inset from *Sports Afield* about how "coyotes, real ones, thrive despite efforts to eliminate them."

39. Christine Mather and Sharon Woods, *Santa Fe Style* (New York: Rizzoli International Publications, 1986), p. 119. The last paragraph of the jacket flap copy reads: "Here is not only the romance of Santa Fe, but the irresistible appeal of its lifestyle—a casual elegance enlivened by a dynamic, ever-changing mixture of the old and the new, the West and the East, the plain and the sophisticated. In addition to the wide range of design ideas offered by the illustrations is a list of sources directing readers to Santa Fe merchants and services." Not surprisingly, Davis Mather Folk Art Gallery and Robert A. Woods Construction, Inc., figure among them.

40. Baca and Deats, *Santa Fe Design*, p. 248.

41. Stephen Parks, "The Southwest Is an Idea," *Southwest Profile*, July, 1988, p. 43. For an indication of Stanley Marcus's views on folk art and its collection and display, see his biographical sketch of "Alexander Girard: Designer and Collector," in Henry Glassie, *The*

Spirit of Folk Art: The Girard Collection at the Museum of International Folk Art (New York: Harry N. Abrams with Santa Fe: Museum of New Mexico, 1989), pp. 11–13. Marcus concludes that Girard's "greatest skill, it seems to me, is his ability to organize diverse objects—whether they be keys, gloves, bills of lading, hinges, or folk art—into intelligible, artistic, and convincing presentations" (p. 13).

42.*Hotel El Tovar*.

43. Babcock, "A New Mexican Rebecca," p. 406. She cited Edward W. Said, *Orientalism* (1978; New York: Vintage Books, 1979), pp. 5-6. Said, in turn, cites K. M. Panikkar, *Asia and Western Dominance* (London: George Allen and Unwin, 1959).

44. Babcock, "A New Mexican Rebecca," pp. 403, 428; anonymous tourist quoted in Hyde, *An American Vision*, p. 241.

45. Helga Teiwes, *Kachina Dolls: The Art of Hopi Carvers* (Tucson: University of Arizona Press, 1991), pp. 42–43, 69–70. For a telling account of commodification and connoisseurship, including "Prices of Dolls," "Doll Mysticism," and a comparison of "Tihus and Santos," see Indian trader Erik Bromberg's *The Hopi Approach to the Art of Kachina Doll Carving* (West Chester, Penn.: Schiffer Pub., 1986).

46. Weigle, *Brothers of Light*, pp. 105–109.

47. Mabel DeLaMater Scacheri, "The Penitentes: Murderous or Misguided?" *Family Circle*, Mar. 20, 1936, p. 15; George Carpenter Baker, *Pachuco: An American-Spanish Argot and Its Social Functions in Tucson, Arizona* (1950; with additions, Tucson: University of Arizona Press, 1958), p. 21. Baker notes that "the word 'pachuco' is a colloquial way of saying El Paso . . . [and] a person from El Paso commonly is referred to as 'Del pachuco.'" He cites claims that the 7-X, a *grifo* gang from the neighborhood of Florence and Eighth Streets, originated Pachuco jargon, likely influenced by "the *Caló* or argot of the Mexican underworld."

48. Ann Vedder, "History of the Spanish Colonial Arts Society, Inc., 1951–1981," in *Hispanic Arts and Ethnohistory in the Southwest: New Papers Inspired by the Work of E. Boyd*, ed. Marta Weigle with Claudia Larcombe and Samuel Larcombe (Albuquerque: University of New Mexico Press; Santa Fe: Ancient City Press, 1983), pp. 210–11. Charles M. Carrillo's full-color, quarter-page ad is in *Spanish Market*, published by the Spanish Colonial Arts Society for the 1992 Spanish Market, Santa Fe, p. 32.

49. George Kubler, "On the Colonial Extinction of the Motifs of Pre-Columbian Art," in *Essays in Pre-Columbian Art and Archeology*, ed. Samuel K. Lothrop et al. (Cambridge: Harvard University Press, 1961), as cited by William Wroth, "Introduction: Hispanic Southwestern Craft Traditions," p. 3.

50. Suzanne Deats and John Villani, *Interior Furnishings Southwest: The Sourcebook of the Best Production Craftspeople* (Santa Fe: John Muir Publications, 1992), p. 28. This September, 1992, compilation proclaims the American Southwest to be "a beacon that draws interest from designers, art collectors, and homeowners around the world [who] are excited by the romance, glamour, and rambunctious humor of the West and by the mystique of the Native American and Hispanic influences that are reflected in the region's graphic design elements" (p. 1). It includes over two hundred predominantly male craftspeople, mostly furniture makers from New Mexico, Arizona, Colorado, Utah, and Wyoming.

51. Jan Best, "Pacheco's Pink Church Isn't—It's a Furniture Gallery," *Santa Fe New Mexican*, June 12, 1991, C-4. Burke and his church and the El Salvadoran workers were photographed by Ann Hunkins, "A Divine Craft," *Santa Fe New Mexican*, Apr. 2, 1993, C-1.

52. On this and others of Milord's work, see Weigle, "Southwest Lures," pp. 503–509.

SYLVIA RODRÍGUEZ

The Tourist Gaze, Gentrification, and the Commodification of Subjectivity in Taos

The eyes have a staring expression; they are always seeking something. What are they seeking? The whites always want something; they are always uneasy and restless. We think that they are mad.

—Ochwiay Biano

Is looking like sucking: the more lookers, the less there is to see?

—Walker Percy

THREE COMPLEMENTARY, interactive cultural-ideological processes have characterized the century-long evolution of a tourism economy in northern New Mexico. The first laid the groundwork for the other two and involves the visual objectification of topography into landscape or scenery, a system of signification constructed for and responsive to the tourist gaze. The tourist gaze in northern New Mexico has, largely through the media of painting and photography, simultaneously projected and fed upon a romantic mix of arid landscape, adobe architecture, and ethnic symbolism. It can be seen to have progressed iconographically from the early days of the Taos painters and Santa Fe railroad to the postmodern veneer of the Santa Fe style. The second process, gentrification, involves the transformation of the built environment into tourist sites embedded within an increasingly elaborate and all-encompassing resort system. The third process, the commodification of subjectivity, refers to the different pathways along which individuals within the tourist setting—including natives—internalize, resist, and reproduce the gaze. All three processes are interactive and have intensified while resort development accelerated into the present. This essay traces the interaction among these three processes from their inception to the 1990s and argues that they reflect both the force and the evolving local face of advanced consumer capitalism.

Critics of the social science literature on tourism have noted the need to distinguish between the impact of tourism on host communities and the effects of urbanization, modernization, or capitalist development in general.[1] In the case of Taos, these phenomena are not entirely separable, empirically or analytically, having gone hand-in-hand from the beginning. Modernization, urbanization, and capitalist development are different aspects of (and ways of talking about) the same process, which in Taos has occurred in the form of tourism. But it may prove useful to try to determine whether there is a particular configuration diagnostic of tourism, in contrast to other forms of economic regime. I propose that in Taos, and therefore in northern New Mexico, the gaze, gentrification, and the commodification of subjectivity define the signature of tourism.

The history of the development of tourism in Taos will first be encapsulated very briefly. The time span under consideration started in the 1890s, after the Santa Fe railway began to use and commission paintings to advertise and when the first art colony painters arrived in Taos. In 1902 the Fred Harvey Company built the Alvarado Hotel in Albuquerque, hiring designer-architect Mary Colter to decorate the interior, thereby creating the prototype for all subsequent Harvey Houses across New Mexico and Arizona.[2] The Taos Society of Artists was founded in 1912. Coke and other art historians hold that the "golden age" of the Taos and Santa Fe art colonies occurred between 1900 and World War II, in three successive phases: a period of early romantic Indianist portraiture ending around the time of statehood in 1912, a "flowering and diversification" era lasting through the 1920s, and a "modernist" phase between the Depression and the war.[3]

Taos's reputation as a bohemian mecca began with the arrival of Mabel Dodge in late 1916. After World War I automobile travel became increasingly important in the region, when Harvey started a car-touring company known as Indian Detours. Tourists reached northern New Mexico mainly by rented car and stayed in local hotels: Harvey's La Fonda in Santa Fe or the Don Fernando in Taos, which although independently built by Gerson Gusdorf must surely have been influenced by Colter's style. The 1930s saw the establishment of tourism as a mainstay of the local economy in both Taos and Santa Fe. Cars became widespread before World War II and universal thereafter, spawning roadside, motel, and strip development.

In sum, Taos has undergone two periods of accelerated tourism development in this century: first, between World War I and World War II;

and second, from the 1960s to the present, with ups and downs during this second, still ongoing, growth phase. During the first of these boom periods, the town established its signature theme as a borderlands Indianist art colony. The second boom involved the rise of the ski industry and a steady march toward massive resort expansion. It followed two postwar decades of slowed economic growth and substantial native emigration for employment. Since the 1960s the Taos real estate market has seen several minor ebbs and flows within its overall surge of steady expansion.

All three of the transformational processes to be discussed here originated during the early phases of the art colony and tourism development. Each has evolved and interacted with the others through time, reflecting larger sociocultural and economic conditions in character and intensity.

THE GAZE

The notion of the gaze as a cultural-ideological construct derives from poststructuralist and feminist analyses of systems of meaning implicit and embedded in paradigmatic structures of power. Today there are at least three common usages of the term: the imperial gaze, the male gaze, and the tourist gaze. All three imply domination, objectification, and a privileging of the visual over other sensory modalities. The gaze in general implies both detachment and a visual semiotic. The idea seems to have originated in Freud's psychoanalytic discussion of erotic looking and scopophilia. Michel Foucault mentioned the gaze in reference to the rise of particular western societal institutions such as the modern prison or medical science, while feminists describe it as a product and instrument of patriarchal domination.[4] The notion of the tourist gaze is implicit in Judith Adler's account of the historical development of sightseeing as well as throughout Dean MacCannell's important discussion of tourism and sight sacralization. The term becomes explicit, although it remains undertheorized, in John Urry's book by the same title.[5]

Adler contended that sightseeing as a tourist practice gradually gained prominence between 1600 and 1800, a period during which "travel method shifted from a scholastic focus upon touring as an opportunity for discourse, to enthusiasm for travel as 'eyewitness' observation. In the course of this shift in attention from the traveller's ear and tongue to the traveller's eye, many of the conventions of sightseeing performance were first developed." The "post-Renaissance secular art of travel," manifest in the grand tour, placed ideological emphasis upon the scientific enumeration and collection of global exotica in order to create an inventory of empirical and historical knowledge. Gradually, however, the "dominant canon of sightseeing changed to serve other intentions," and "the traveler's 'eye,' hitherto bound by a normative discourse rooted to fealty in science, became increasingly subject to a new discipline of connoisseurship. The well-trained 'eye' judiciously attributed works of art, categorized them by style, and made authoritative judgments of aesthetic merit, as travel itself became an occasion for the cultivation and display of 'taste.' "[6] The grand tour, or journey, in search of knowledge thus became, by the end of the eighteenth century, a more leisurely pursuit of the picturesque, in which aesthetic experience assumed priority.

Adler looked at these modes of perception in relation to their changing historical context. She noted "the fit between a form of travel which featured the world as a series of 'things' to be objectively enumerated, and acts of appropriation which lifted such things from the contexts in which they were found in order to complete collections of things elsewhere." Referring to the change that had emerged by the nineteenth century, Adler commented:

> One is tempted to suspect as well that during the period in which, for the first time, a single system of interrelated markets began to span the globe, a style of travel performance which privileged the eye for comprehensive inventory served as one of the rituals through which European cultural and intellectual elites sought to take title to "the whole world" then coming into view. The form of human subjectivity such travel ritual required, honed, and exalted was one which could "grasp" this vast new world of "things" without being overwhelmed by it.[7]

This "panoramization of the world" came to characterize European modes of perception during the industrial transformation. It contrasted with preindustrial modes wherein the traveler was immersed in and therefore engaged with the environment or countryside. The visual aestheticization of travel was also broadly contemporaneous with the rise of painting as a prestigious and popular art form.[8] The artistic subject matter itself would mirror the changing character of the gaze.

A recursive relation between the visual arts and the tourist gaze is readily apparent in the Southwest, where painting and photography simultaneously reflect and project the tourist gaze in its purest form. For the tourist, the Southwest was, from the beginning, a predominantly visual or scenic experience: transient, achieved through industrial travel, and mediated by painters and photographers. The first view of the landscape through a train compartment window profoundly influenced how travelers would perceive and conceptualize the physical and social world beyond the train. Wolfgang Schivelbusch noted how railroad travel "created a new landscape" by virtue of "the moving window which made it seem as if the landscape itself were moving."

> The railroad choreographed the landscape. The motion of the train shrank space, and this displayed an immediate succession of objects and pieces of scenery that in their original spatiality belong to separate realms. The traveller who gazed through the compartment window at such successive scenes, acquired a novel ability that Gastineau calls "la philosophie synthétique du coup d'oeil" (the synthetic philosophy of the glance). It was the ability to perceive the discrete, as it rolls past the window, indiscriminately.[9]

The tourist gaze in New Mexico exhibits two defining features: predominance of what Urry called the romantic gaze and symbolic fixation on Indians. Urry distinguished between the collective and romantic forms of the tourist gaze. Whereas the collective gaze derives its appeal from an experience of collective or shared viewing of a given spectacle, the romantic gaze emphasizes an experience of "solitude, privacy, and a personal, semi-spiritual relationship with the object of the gaze."[10] Nothing conveys the ethos of the gaze better than the paintings themselves, except perhaps the artists' own words. Consider, for example, the arrival narrative of Ernest Blumenschein (Taos art colony co-founder): "My grunting horse carried me down and across the gorges, around the foothills, over long flat spaces that were like great lakes of sagebrush through twenty slow miles of thrilling sensation. It had to end in the Taos valley, green with trees and fields of alfalfa, populated by dark-skinned people who greeted me pleasantly. Then I saw my first Taos Indians, picturesque, colorful, dressed in blankets artistically draped. New Mexico had gripped me."[11] Compare Mabel Dodge's memory of her first view of the Taos Pueblo:

> We finally came along close to the mountain. It swept away above us, and there at the foot of it was the Pueblo . . . on either side of a sparkling brown stream that rushed down from a canyon . . . two big community houses were standing in a smooth, clear space of earth, absolutely stark and undecorated. . . . Now, strange to say, although the village seemed austere and certainly anything but domestic, yet one got a feeling of home from it. Why? I do not

> know. That was the feeling it gave out richly. A stab of longing and of nostalgia went through me like lightning.[12]

This yearning motivated a lifelong stay for virtually all of the early art colonists. They saw in Taos an exotic, pristine world that assumed shape and meaning in contrast to the urban industrial world they tried to escape. As Bert Phillips wrote, explaining why he never returned to his previous home:

> Sometimes I ask myself why I remain away from the "Land of Civilization" but never before have I tried to formulate a reply. I have simply been content to stay on. The charm of the great stretches of mountain and plains and the interest of their inhabitants is never ending. As I visit their villages and talk with my Indian friends, I see and hear the young bucks standing on the bridge singing a love song in the moonlight, and I feel the romance of youth, so the answer comes as I write and I believe that it is the romance of this great pure-aired land that makes the most lasting impression on my mind and heart.[13]

These examples reveal several things. To begin with, the art colonists extolled a sense of immediacy and spatial engulfment associated with pre-industrial rather than train travel, but nonetheless enabled by the latter and valorized by virtue of the contrast between them. The artists' intensely visualist perspective was pierced with longing for a premodern, more "authentic" world. Because the railroad never penetrated the town, Taos provided a travel experience that depended upon and yet eluded the industrial reach, the growing role of the automobile notwithstanding. It is worth noting that probably the supreme recreational activity of the early artists and company, other than gazing at Indian dances, was to rent horses or wagons to ride all over the countryside around Taos. The art colony's origin myth—of Blumenschein and Phillips' broken wagon wheel carried into town for repair—dramatizes the poignant impulse to stray beyond the frontier to a remote, semi-wild world yet unruined by civilization. The solitary quintessence of the romantic gaze in New Mexico was captured by Charles F. Lummis's popular phrase, "sun, silence, and adobe," or later on by almost any O'Keeffe landscape. Urry linked the romantic gaze to the spread of global tourism as well as to a middle- instead of a working-class clientele, an association confirmed by its source in New Mexico among an elite sector of urban expatriots.[14]

The gaze and its scenery comprise ideological work as well as material reproduction, and they involve certain social arrangements. The early Taos painters invented the town's dominant symbol, the "adobe-nature complex": an image of one or more adobe buildings, such as the multistoried Taos Pueblo, cast against a mountain backdrop.[15] This image contains the major elements—landscape, adobe architecture, and (implicitly) Indians—of the regional visual semiotic. Variations of the adobe-nature complex are endlessly reproduced in photographs, paintings, postcards, souvenirs, memorabilia, and trinkets emblematic of the region.

This process of tourist site development and autoinscription resembles what John Dorst described for the tourist site of Chadds Ford, Pennsylvania, where "a unified landscape or consistent visual experience is influenced by a particular visual rhetoric, a uniform way of seeing that begins in the handling point-of-view in Brandywine School [substitute Taos art colony] paintings—especially Andrew Wyeth's [substitute Ernest Blumenschein, Joseph Sharp, Bert Phillips, or E. Irving Couse]—and the postcards available to tourists, and extends to the control of vantage point in everyday life."[16]

Although the historical particulars for Taos and Chadds Ford differ, the process by which each evolved into a postmodern tourist site over roughly the same period of time seems almost identical. The precise nature of this metamorphosis nevertheless remains somewhat elusive. Dorst wrote that "an act of distancing makes scenery out of topography, but what complicated ideological processes allow one to experience scenery through the categories of pictorial art? And even more perplexing, what transformation makes specific paintings the legitimizing antecedents of the physical locales they depict, so that the attraction of these geographical sites is their offer of participation in the painted images?"[17]

It is with respect to people or human subjects—or objects—that the asymmetrical relationship between the gazer and the gazed upon becomes most important. Part of what is striking about the tourism industry in New Mexico is its ingenious use of a deeply rooted system of ethnic stratification long persistent under conditions of economic underdevelopment. A discourse of representation instigated through art became the key mechanism whereby the obvious social and economic liabilities of the region were converted into touristic assets. Indians have always been the primary human subject matter of southwestern painting and photography, with Mexicans and cowboys running a distant second and third. This aesthetic hierarchy symbolically inverts the actual colonial and postcolonial order, in which Indians generally occupy the bottom rung. Mexicans are above them, and gringo cowboys are lower-class members of the top ethnic stratum.

Indian imagery is as prevalent today as in the early 1900s, although the style of representation has changed in significant ways. The overall visual-aesthetic trend since World War II has been toward decorative stylization on the one hand and extreme photorealism on the other, as well as the mass proliferation of ethnic symbols in general. If one were to systematically compare artistic images from successive decades, a trend toward ever-greater mechanical reproducibility would be easily apparent.

Feminist deconstruction of the male gaze as an instrument of sex-gender hegemony points to several interrelated aspects of the system: physical domination and control, material ownership, appropriation of services, and above all the power of symbolic representation. Although the role of eroticism in the tourist and male gazes may differ, the two are nevertheless comparable in these specific respects.[18] First the artists and ultimately any visitor with a camera cast their hegemonic gaze upon New Mexico, rendering it into an image, an ethos: a place to be visited, owned, bought, and sold. The transformational impact of the gaze upon the landscape and built environment was immense.

GENTRIFICATION: FROM SIGHT SACRALIZATION TO SITE AUTOINSCRIPTION

> Given the emphasis on tourist consumption as visual, and the significance of buildings as objects upon which the gaze is directed, it is essential to consider changing patterns and forms that those buildings might take.[19]

The initial process by which the tourist gaze transforms the attraction or site was described by MacCannell as sight sacralization, which occurs in several stages: naming, framing and elevation, enshrinement, mechanical reproduction, and social reproduction.[20] Tourist attractions thereby become settings for staged authenticity. Sight sacralization casts a new net of meanings over the topography in question. My main interest here is in what happens to a tourist site through time, especially as practitioners of the gaze become its entrenched mediators and promoters.

Lawrence Moss applied the term *amenity migrant* to those who first come as tourists and then remain, either permanently or for extended periods, or who return for life on a seasonal basis.[21] A special term for this group is useful for two reasons: first, to distinguish between such former tourists and the regular tourists just passing through; and second, because this population happens to supply the largest proportion of local tourism entrepreneurs and business owners. Their significant internal differentiation notwithstanding, amenity migrants are the major agents of local tourism promotion and development. The establishment of tourism as a mainstay of the local economy generated its own self-sustaining elite. This constituency became, in cooperation with the state, the dominant agent of site autoinscription.

The original amenity migrants were the art colonists, who inaugurated the unending stream of outsiders drawn to New Mexico precisely because of its exotic-nostalgic appeal. A curious trait of amenity migrants is that although they constitute a major source of local change, they nevertheless hold the greatest stake in trying to prevent visible change, which they often openly oppose. Indeed, the most elite sectors of the amenity migrant population have always been strong, persuasive, and highly vocal proponents of selective ethnocultural and environmental conservation and preservation. Like every population, they are internally divided by class as well as by other competing interests.

Such transplants assumed an active role in the incorporation of Taos as a town in 1934, and they have continued to exert considerable influence over various aspects of civic as well as commercial life ever since. Amenity migrants give impetus and direction to the touristic autoinscription of Taos. Their modus operandi includes what MacCannell called "museumization," whereby the modern or touristic sensibility tries to recover or "preserve" the premodern.

Architectural transformation registers Taos's growth and progressive elaboration as a tourist attraction. The art colonists and subsequent amenity migrants sought to preserve the adobe look. Before World War II, this was accomplished with "unskilled" local labor in adobe construction and maintenance. After World War II, cinderblock and frame with stucco gradually supplanted adobe construction. In the contemporary period dating from the 1960s, new (as well as restorative) adobe construction has become almost exclusively the prerogative of affluent amenity migrants and occasionally of native elites. An adobe visual rhetoric, whose "legitimizing antecedents" are seen in regional paintings and photographs, still prevails across the full architectural spectrum, dictating everything from cheap look-alike to costly "postpueblo revival." Like Chadds Ford, Taos took on "that paradoxical quality of being both a place where people actually live and an idea of a way of life, represented mainly by the preservation, or wholesale creation, of the appropriate look. The controlling idea is that one will actually live at the vantage point from which the paintings are painted and the postcards photographed."[22]

Because the downtown plaza areas of both Taos and Santa Fe have been the original and most intense loci of site autoinscription, each offers a diachronic window into the evolution of this process, decade by decade, from modern to postmodern stages. One obvious trend is the gradual transformation of both plazas from local commercial centers, featuring a range of services and products for the local populace, to theme malls for specialty shopping by tourists. The dry-goods stores, cantinas, barber shops, cafes, and offices of a generation ago have been supplanted entirely by art galleries, boutiques, and souvenir shops, a transition made absolute during the 1980s. Although the number of plaza businesses may have multiplied over the decades, their variety has diminished. Today local residents have little reason to visit the plaza and tend to avoid it. They conduct their regular shopping in large franchise stores located along the "strip" south of town.

This transformation of the plaza is concurrent with other startling changes in the built environment and in property ownership and use in and around the town. The term *gentrification* seems to apply here. Gentrification is defined by sociologists and planning theorists as "the rehabilitation of working-class inner-city neighborhoods for upper-middle class consumption."[23] Although generally regarded as a deep urban or inner-city phenomenon, the process known as gentrification seems to be what is happening in and around Taos concurrent with resort development. Taos, although certainly urbanizing, is not urban in the technical sense of the word. That it is undergoing gentrification is therefore perhaps less a function of its degree of urbanization than of a general stage of capital development.

> Gentrification is an international phenomenon occurring simultaneously in many cities—and at a specific period in the history of capitalism. In other words, after a long period in which their dominant function was to assist in the production of labor power, many neighborhoods are now being used for their alternative function—as commodities or groups of commodities, the production, consumption, and reproduction of which are a source of profit for certain members of the capitalist class. At least for the moment, the economic function of neighborhood has superseded the broader social function.[24]

Most real estate development around Taos involves the renovation of existing adobe structures in addition to new construction in previously uninhabited areas. In the former category, rural housing vacated by emigrating families was typically rented and eventually sold to amenity migrants eager and easily able to own a piece of Taos. Inside the town most real estate is now owned by Anglo amenity migrants, although a number of native landowners have managed to hold onto and in some cases develop their property. Outside the town, within and between the numerous satellite villages, second homes, subdivisions, and condominiums proliferate, unregulated by any form of county zoning code. The diagnostica of this boom include a steady rise in real estate prices, coupled with frequent turnover and a trend away from Hispano toward greater amenity-migrant or outside ownership. Also evident are escalating resort and second-home construction.[25] Several factors promote native emigration and make it hard for Hispanos to hold onto their land, while simultaneously fostering amenity immigration. Local conditions include limited (mostly government or tourism-generated) employment opportunities, high unemployment, low per capita income, a resort-inflated cost of living, and a pronounced wealth differential between natives and amenity migrants and tourists.

Gentrification is identifiable as a distinct kind of upscale, aesthetically pleasing renovation of earlier architectural structures and styles, in this case adobe or adobelike. It is happening in areas previously occupied but for the most part no longer owned by native Hispanos, who moved out—sometimes to mobile homes, to low-income housing in the vicinity, or to cities in search of employment. Whereas gentrification of the plaza and central district of the town was not typically preceded by abandonment, this is sometimes the case in outlying placitas, such as the nearby La Loma plaza or the Ranchos plaza to the south. Either way, according to Smith and LaFaivre, the cause is the same.

> It is clear that displacement due to abandonment has exactly the same cause as so-called gentrification-caused displacement. It is simply displacement one stage earlier; in an area to be gentrified, the residents are displaced before gentrification begins rather than directly by the gentrifiers. Even when abandonment is not followed by gentrification, displacement results from the same cycle of economic events that produces gentrification and has the same effect on the displaced population.[26]

In sum, gentrification consists of demographic displacement/replacement of a poorer population by a wealthier one and a concomitant physical transformation/intensification of the built environment. In Taos, this process is situated within a still-emerging resort system that is both local-regional and international in scale. The system is emergent because it is still expanding at each of these levels, while their interarticulation continues to ramify and stabilize.

Urry noted that architectural practice is of major importance in shaping the contemporary tourist gaze and suggested that its impact depends upon whether we are dealing with public or private buildings. He asserted that "tourists are socially differentiated and hence gaze selectively upon these different architectural styles."[27] The social composition of the people living in tourist sites, like that of the tourists themselves, is also crucial in shaping how the built environment evolves. Thus the 1990s restoration of the main building complexes at the Taos Pueblo, financed by a combination of federal and private funding, promises to expand the scope and meaning of gentrification in the Taos area. The renovated edifice will be both the same and yet utterly different from before, inscribed with the imprimatur of its own reflexive self-preservation. Such transformation of place involves a transformation of self.

THE COMMODIFICATION OF SUBJECTIVITY

Edward Bruner proposed that despite the common assumption that travel transforms the traveler, modern tourist experiences and settings are geared to the convenience of the customer and strive to minimize the need for any adjustment or change.[28] Required instead are massive adjustments and changes on the part of host or native populations. Every possible position on both sides of the great guest / host divide entails a particular perspective and experience worthy of investigation. But my primary interest is on what happens to the host population through time, especially to "ethnic natives" in a postcolonial tourist mecca like Taos.

A remarkable painting by art colonist Oscar Berninghaus, entitled *Joe in the Studio*, shows a well-known Taos Pueblo man with braids, standing in front of the artist's palette. He gazes directly at the viewer, grinning. One can only guess what Berninghaus meant to say about Joe and, by implication, their relationship. For a philosopher, the notion of a return gaze might evoke Sartre's claims about the complex existential ramifications of "the look and the look back" between two individual consciousnesses.[29]

But though the painting might seem at first glance to portray the Other's subjectivity (the Indian as he "really" is, possibly even wearing the artist's hand-me-down clothes), by implication engaging the artist's subjectivity, what it literally depicts is the native Other as the artist's subordinate.

My own reading suggests that the scene also captures the purely hypothetical origin point of the commodification of subjectivity for the Taos Indian: the moment the model steps behind the easel and sees, for the first time, what the artist sees—his/her own image in the artist's eyes. One can read into Joe's expression the mixture of bemusement, recognition, disbelief, shock, repugnance, amusement, and odd elation this touristic primordial scene might engender. The painting, in fact, shows not the very moment but a subsequent one. This is never a single moment, of course, but an ongoing and evolving situation or condition. It also suggests that the native too has a gaze, portrayed here as a gazing back.

Just as internal colonization involves a process whereby the colonized see themselves and their kind as the debased rabble the colonizer sees, so does the touristic commodification of native subjectivity entail the experience of beholding oneself or one's own as the object of the romantic tourist gaze. But this is a much more complex psychological "moment" than the prerequisite colonizing instance, because it combines contradictory elements of empowerment with yet a new form of subjugation. Thereafter both resistance and capitulation are interwoven in the native's return gaze.

On the one hand, the native is seduced by his own glamorous image in the admiring eyes of the friendly new colonizers. He gains crucial insight into the Other's exploitable yearning. On the other hand, the new economy of authenticity offers fresh opportunity—perilous in its combination of allure and illusion. Once he has stepped behind the easel, so to speak, the native is caught in a constant tension between being controlled (taken in or trapped) by his romanticized image, on the one hand, and having control over and being able to use it effectively, on the other. Successful manipulation of the image without succumbing to it is a tricky and dangerous business that requires a delicate mix of skepticism, separatism, and at least qualified good faith. This creates a split, I propose, between the self offered up to or hunted down by the tourist gaze and the self who tries to live where the gaze cannot penetrate.

The situation in Taos thus has encouraged a kind of dual or double ethnicity in both colonized groups, by which natives have come to enact and recognize a distinction between cultural practice for themselves and cultural practice exposed to the all-consuming tourist gaze. As Lynn Stephen observed with reference to a comparable dual or multidimensional ethnicity among contemporary Zapotec weavers, "One face is shown to consumers of indigenous culture (such as tourists, importers, state agencies, and foreigners who purchase indigenous crafts), and another operates within [the community] and is accessible to those who are members . . . by virtue of their participation in local networks and institutions."[30] Professional ethnicity first arose in the modeling situation or relation, which combined—or alternated—posing or "sitting" with menial household service, the arrangement depicted in Berninghaus's painting. From there it sprouted a thousand different Hydra heads among all sectors and strata of the local Indian and Hispano populations. Indians and Mexicanos are differently positioned within the political economy, and their opportunities and strategies have varied accordingly. Over many decades, tourism has fostered pseudoethnicity among tourist and amenity-migrant "wannabes" and has glamorized defensive, dual, and intensified hyperethnicity among various native sectors.[31]

The point is not that natives sold out to tourism but that individuals as well as groups respond to its inescapable advance in different, complex, and often contradictory ways. Today, a few resist it outright while others quite consciously pair outward compliance with private grumbling or small acts of sabotage. A significant proportion endorses, promotes, and participates in the official protourism position. Most Taoseños, and even amenity migrants, express a sense of powerlessness and frustration about their ability to change the existing situation or to "stop progress." Thus there are multiple pathways into commodified subjectivity and myriad ways in which people resist the process of commodification. Each individual journey originates at a specific locale and involves a particular, often meandering, trajectory. But beneath the diversity is the dynamic, inherently conflicted nature of the process itself—both within and between groups, sectors, and individuals. As Bruner noted, "The hegemonic does not imply complete consensus or naive acceptance, for . . . there are always some segments of society with alternate views who question the hegemonic. The hegemonic is always striving, always in process."[32] At the personal level, it is a process of constant struggle. Individuals become living, breathing, mobile, yet frequently trapped zones of contestation between counter-hegemonic resistance and commodifying subjectivity. Eventually, everyone becomes divided over the issue of escalating resort development. The inner battle over commodification is apparent wherever one looks in tourist towns like Taos or Santa Fe. It is waged across amenity-migrant as well as native sectors.

I will now move from the notion of how individual native subjectivity first becomes seduced and divided by the tourist gaze to a consideration of group-level phenomena observed at later, more advanced, stages of the process. In making this shift, some intermediate conceptual terrain must be left behind, at least for the moment. This includes a comparative examination of individual narratives, which must belong to a separate discussion focused specifically on subjective mechanisms of resistance. Part of this territory has been covered elsewhere in some detail. It concerns the major ways in which Indian and Hispano/Mexicano experiences, perspectives, and boundary maintenance strategies have differed in Taos during successive stages of tourism development.[33]

One response Indians and Hispanos do have in common, however, is the emergence of defensive cultural conservatism and preservationism among their own elite and middle classes. The following section will address two general features of how this reactive growth of conservation-preservation activism has unfolded among Hispanos during the past twenty-five years. I refer to these phenomena as "surface politics," in implied contrast to the "deep politics" of individual subjective reaction and maneuvering within the touristic situation.[34] These surface politics reflect, at the group level, the progression of and struggle against the commodification of subjectivity.

THE SURFACE POLITICS OF CONSERVATIONISM

Urry identified three elements in the relationship between local areas and tourism development: local people who wish to conserve features of the environment that symbolize the lived locality, a variety of private-sector owners and potential owners of tourist-related services, and the local state.[35] Each of these sectors is found in Taos, where the first two are significantly divided by ethnicity, class, and the distinction between natives and amenity migrants. Linking expansion of the service and middle classes to conservationism, Urry proposed that the localization or low rate of mobility among at least the male service class strengthens conservation movements because "such people are likely to develop more of an attachment to the place than previously."[36] In Taos the localization or low mobility of the service class has different patterns and causes in the case of each ethnic group. Indians, Hispanos, and amenity migrants find themselves in Taos under very different conditions and faced with very different options. Nevertheless, conservation activists exist in all three groups and tend to belong to the service or middle and upper-middle class.

It is significant, then, that the local state tends to be ethnically more homogeneous than either the conservationists or the entrepreneurs. Local government comprises predominantly the Mexicano male service class and has traditionally provided an important if limited avenue of mobility for individuals into or within that sector. Moreover, the local state is least divided when it comes to the overarching issue of accelerating resort development throughout the Taos basin. Town and county government are consistently firm in their support and facilitation of the massive resort development, despite the recent proliferation of opposition by a variety of ethnic, interethnic, and environmental conservationist interests. This attests to the colonial character of the politics of tourism in Taos. It is common enough for municipal and county governments to accommodate to powerful internal as well as external business interests, but local states are dominated by ethnic minorities only in colonial and postcolonial settings. Because the real economic power in Taos is concentrated in the hands of Anglos, this amounts to a kind of indirect rule. It makes for a complexly convoluted dynamic whereby Mexicanos suffer secondary sociocultural and economic status but nevertheless control local politics.

Movements originate differently among different groups. Among amenity migrants, the perennial motivation for conservationism is the romantic gaze. Yearners and tourism entrepreneurs have a straightforward stake in perpetuating a certain look to the place. At Taos Pueblo, boundary defense and resistance to European assimilation began early, evolved through two subsequent regimes, and cannily accommodated to tourism during the twentieth century. Resistance and accommodation become intertwined as tribal members maneuver to protect pueblo life from encroachment, exploitation, and prying while at the same time garnering support by virtue of the same tourist gaze. Hispanos in Taos and its surrounding communities have also resisted and accommodated to Anglo encroachment and domination, holding ground through sheer numbers and tenacious control of the local (municipal and county) electoral politics. While Indian and Anglo perspectives emerge at the opposite extremes of power and resistance, Mexicano vantages emanate from the churning, uneven ground between them.

Cultural and environmental conservation movements have developed among all three ethnic groups in Taos and constitute perhaps the major zone of alliance between them, or their cultural elites, at different times and locations. Regardless of whether it was so intended, the effects of conservation are pleasing to the tourist gaze and in this respect adaptive to a tourism economy. This does not mean, however, they originally emerge as protourist—on the contrary, they often start as some form of protest or overt resistance to a perceived negative change brought about by external forces. Herein lies the contradiction at the heart of the battle waged across the spectrum of local society in tourist centers like Taos. Although conservationist movements oppose urban intensification, they are also an inherent part of its macroprocess. The process seems to unfold as a kind of progressive co-optation. The great paradox of tourism development is that like capitalism itself, it both engenders and consumes its own opposition.

Ethnic boundaries and ethnic politics have intensified as the demographics in Taos shift. The Anglo population of Taos County increased from 6 percent to 20 percent between 1970 and 1980 and grew more during the following decade. The precise number of natives who emigrate every year in search of work or education remains uncounted, as does the number of amenity migrants who arrive to take their place. Resort expansion in and around the town intensifies demand on already overallocated surface and ground waters, upon various kinds of land, and upon certain coveted scenic locales. Ski resorts attract tourists whose wealth is in extreme contrast to the normal means of most natives. Within this context, grassroots *acequia*-based (*acequias* are community irrigation ditch systems) resistance to resort expansion and parish-based religious-cultural revivals emerged during the 1970s and 1980s.[37] They were organized by different elements within the same general class of rural, landholding Hispanos.

Although *acequia*-based protests in the Rio Hondo watershed have tended to be organized by *parciantes* (irrigation water-rights owners) willing to side with Anglo environmentalists, the parish-based revivals appear to be instigated by somewhat more conservative and elite elements who are also *parciantes* but who oppose the resort protests. Both appeal to the same wider audience. The significance of the contrast between their organizing constituencies will be discussed shortly. But first an additional factor must be mentioned, namely, the chronological order in which these popular movements have occurred. In the Taos basin, a protest-revival-gentrification sequence is observable in the Rio Grande del Rancho and Rio Hondo watersheds. These are the two largest watersheds south and north of the town and the sites of densest settlement and growth.

Grassroots protest, *acequia*-based yet ethnically mixed, against a proposed conservancy district and resort-oriented dam project (known as Indian Camp Dam) emerged in the Rio Grande del Rancho watershed during the early 1970s.[38] In the aftermath of the proposed dam's defeat, the San Francisco de Assisi parish, based in Ranchos de Taos, entered a phase of religious-cultural revivalism. This was signaled by a community decision to restore and maintain adobe plaster on their famous mission church and by renewed participation in religious pilgrimage and ritual folk dramas (*Las Posadas, Los Comanches*), as well as in the *Hermandad* or Penitente Brotherhood. During the late 1980s, after roughly two decades of gradual decline and quasi-abandonment, the Ranchos plaza began to undergo gentrification into an attractively restored soft-plaster shopping site for tourists. Today it houses art galleries, boutiques, and other tourist-oriented (and amenity-migrant–owned) enterprises. The other major cultural-institutional presence on the placita remains the Catholic parish office and the monumental church itself.

The Rio Hondo watershed six or more miles north of Taos is the major locus of the ski industry and related secondary resort development in the Taos basin. Grassroots, *acequia*-based protest against pollution of the Rio Hondo by a ski resort emerged more or less contemporaneously with the Indian Camp Dam protest in the early 1970s. But it grew into a much more ambivalent and protracted controversy, involving sporadic mobilization against continuous resort expansion throughout the watershed.[39]

At the same time, the Holy Trinity parish has, like the Saint Francis parish, also experienced ethnoreligious revivals of folk dramas such as *Los Pastores, El Niño Perdido*, and the Matachines dance. The Nuestra Señora de los Dolores chapel in upper Arroyo Hondo more or less simultaneously underwent restoration. Arroyo Seco, the parish seat bisected by the main road to the ski valley, shows advancing signs of gentrification. It has a vaguely Swiss alpine cast, in keeping with the stylistic ethos of the sport.

It is significant that the organizational foci of protest and religious forms of ethnic mobilization seem to be more or less mutually exclusive in the Rio Hondo watershed. The very families who have organized the parish revivals have been internal opponents of the protests. The social distinction between these two organizing constituencies appears along a subtle line of status and class orientation instead of simple class position, with respect to value orientation if not to actual wealth or the holding of land (and therefore water) rights. The ambiguous, even elusive, nature of this contrast underscores the need to attend carefully to internal differentiation between and within classes as well as ethnic groups. Time will tell whether these two forms of ethnic activism prove competitive or merely sequential. In any case, they appear complementary at the level of ethnic boundary maintenance.

Although both forms of activism are reactive to resort development, at least at first glance they appear differentially adaptive to it. Cultural-religious revivalism, organized in Arroyo Seco by a conservative elite, symbolically asserts an ethnic boundary in a way that is nonthreatening to the status quo and appeals outright to the touristic sensibility. At the same time, it fulfills internal needs of ethnic self-affirmation, and its participants would not only deny but take offense at the suggestion that they were touristically motivated. Protest, on the other hand, asserts a territorial boundary threatening to the business establishment. It can highlight internal as well as intergroup divisions even while it momentarily unites and empowers the dissident. But in the long run, protest conservationism also proves adaptive to tourism, inasmuch as its successful outcome satisfies the gaze. So whether native conservationism in either form succeeds or fails, resistance to commodification seems both inherent in the situation and yet itself destined to become another commodity. It reasserts long-standing ethnic boundaries and imparts new meanings for those on either side of them.

CONCLUSION

The tourist gaze, like the gentrification it spawns, ultimately consumes its own opposition. It also calls forth the native object's gaze in response and engenders a split in native subjectivity. This split fuels resistance on the one hand and capitulation on the other, reactions joined in a dynamic dialectical relationship parallel to that between opposition and commodification. The split in native subjectivity is not unique to Taos. Nor is the gradual journey from resistance and ritual performance into commodity, a process seen also in the evolution of Chadds Ford Days from a protest event to an annual living history crafts fair. But the case of Taos differs from Dorst's Chadds Ford or Urry's coastal Britain in that it constitutes a "Fourth World" setting. As an enclaved ethnic minority or postcolonial refuge region within a modern nation-state, it partakes of the First World, or core, while sharing features with the Third World, or periphery. In Taos, the host-guest distinction is compounded by divisions of ethnicity as well as class. The pressures created by amenity migration and resort expansion intensify the crosscutting lines of oppositional and competitive interests that define local politics. The macrosocial forces of tourism collide with their opposition at microsites within and between individuals in all ethnic groups, arising constantly and lending movement to historical process experienced as daily life. Different locations within the major groups give rise to particular sorts of contradictions and tensions. Along with expressive culture and the built environment, these struggles leave clear tracks and should constitute a major focus for the ethnographic study of a tourist site.

NOTES

This paper was originally prepared for the plenary session of the annual meeting of the Society for Cultural Anthropology, held in Austin, Texas, on May 15, 1992. It was subsequently presented at the annual meeting of the American Ethnological Society held in Santa Fe, New Mexico, on April 17, 1993. The research on which it is based was assisted by support from the Southwest Hispanic Research Institute and the Center for Regional Studies, at the University of New Mexico. I am grateful to Marta Weigle, Jose Limón, Robert Paul, and Douglas Foley for critical comments on earlier versions of this paper.

The chapter epigraphs are from Ochwiay Biano of Taos Pueblo to C. G. Jung, in Carl G. Jung, *Memories, Dreams, Reflections*, Aniela Jaffe, ed. (New York: Pantheon Books, 1963), p. 248; and Walker Percy, "The Loss of the Creature," in *Message in the Bottle: How Queer Man Is, How Queer Language Is, and What One Has to Do with the Other* (New York: Farrar, Straus and Giroux, 1975), p. 49.

1. Malcolm Crick, "Representations of International Tourism in the Social Sciences: Sun, Sex, Sights, Savings, and Servility," *Annual Review of Anthropology* 18 (1989): 307–44.

2. Marta Weigle, "Exposition and Mediation: Mary Colter, Erna Fergusson, and the Santa Fe/Harvey Popularization of the Native Southwest, 1902–1940," *Frontiers: A Journal of Women's Studies* 12, no. 3 (1992): 117–50.

3. V. D. Coke, *Taos and Santa Fe: The Artist's Environment, 1882–1942* (Albuquerque: University of New Mexico Press, 1963).

4. Laura Mulvey, *Visual and Other Pleasures* (Bloomington and Indianapolis: Indiana University Press, 1975), p. 16; Michel Foucault, *The Birth of the Clinic* (London: Tavistock, 1976); Michel Foucault, *Discipline and Punish* (New York: Vintage Books, 1979). For femi-

nist views see Mulvey, *Visual and Other Pleasures*; Marilyn Frye, *The Politics of Reality: Essays in Feminist Theory* (New York: Crossing Press, 1983); E. Ann Kaplan, "Is the Gaze Male?" in *Powers of Desire: The Politics of Sexuality*, Snitow et al., eds. (New York: Feminist Press, 1983), pp. 309–27.

5. Judith Adler, "The Origins of Sightseeing," *Annals of Tourism Research* 16 (1989): 7–29; Dean MacCannell, *The Tourist* (New York: Schocken Books, 1976); John Urry, *The Tourist Gaze* (New York: Sage Publications, 1990).

6. Adler, "Origins of Sightseeing," pp. 7, 22.

7. Ibid., p. 24.

8. Ibid., p. 22.

9. Wolfgang Schivelbusch, *The Railway Journey: The Industrialization of Time and Space in the Nineteenth Century* (Berkeley: University of California Press, 1986), pp. 60–61.

10. Urry, *The Tourist Gaze*, p. 45.

11. Quotes are in Sandra D'Emilio and Suzan Campbell, *Visions and Visionaries: The Art and Artists of the Santa Fe Railway* (Salt Lake City: Peregrine-Smith Books, 1991), p. 55.

12. Ibid., p. 99.

13. Ibid., p. 80.

14. Urry, *The Tourist Gaze*, pp. 46–47.

15. Etsuko Kuroda, *Ethnicity and Ethnic Crisis: The Struggle for Existence of the Spanish-American in Taos, New Mexico* (Osaka: National Museum of Ethnology, 1981).

16. John Dorst, *The Written Suburb* (Philadelphia: University of Pennsylvania Press, 1989), p. 29.

17. Ibid., p. 57.

18. See Barbara Babcock's work on olla maidens, or popular images of Pueblo women with pottery jars on their heads, for an analysis of the intersection between the tourist gaze and the male gaze in the U.S. Southwest: Babcock, "'A New Mexican Rebecca': Imaging Pueblo Women," *Journal of the Southwest* 32, no. 4 (1990): 400-37. See also "Mudwomen and Whitemen: A Meditation on Pueblo Potteries and the Politics of Representation," in *The Material Culture of Gender / The Gender of Material Culture*, Kenneth Ames and Katherine Martinez, eds. (New York: W. W. Norton and Co., 1991).

19. Urry, *The Tourist Gaze*, p. 120.

20. MacCannell, *The Tourist*, pp. 44–45.

21. Lawrence Moss, "Amenity Migration," unpublished paper (1991).

22. Dorst, *The Written Suburb*, pp. 32–33. My work calls attention to the importance of the built environment as a feature of tourism's evolving hegemony in Taos, but it does not attempt to examine precisely how this process took place or what it looked like at different points in history. For such a study of Santa Fe, see Chris Wilson, *The Myth of Santa Fe: Tourism, Ethnic Identity, and the Creation of a Modern Regional Culture* (Albuquerque: University of New Mexico Press, in press). Wilson's architectural history of that city describes in detail how the transformation of the built environment progressed through different political, economic, and sociocultural regimes. He traces how the architecture of Santa Fe has changed over generations and who the key figures and institutions were in creating the complex of images and structures called Santa Fe style. The case of Santa Fe is instructive because, although differing from it in significant ways, Taos is nevertheless located within the capital city's political and economic orbit and has always been influenced by its cultural trends.

23. Neil Smith and Michele LaFaivre, "A Class Analysis of Gentrification," in *Gentrification, Displacement, and Neighborhood Revitalization*, J. John Palen and Bruce London, eds. (Albany: State University of New York Press), p. 43.

24. Ibid., p. 46.

25. The terms *Hispano* and *Mexicano* are used here more or less interchangeably to refer to the genetically mestizo, Spanish-speaking native population of northern New Mexico. Although these two terms have different connotations, both are generally acceptable to the people in question when speaking in English and Spanish, respectively. Except for *Mexicano* when speaking in Spanish, perhaps only the term *La Raza* or *Raza* approaches universal acceptance as an ethnic self-referent among this general population. The genteel term in English has for many decades been "Spanish" or "Spanish American" and is today considered objectionable by a younger generation of self-identified Chicanos. The term *Chicano*, however, remains unpopular among many calling themselves Spanish or Spanish American.

26. Smith and LaFaivre, "Class Analysis of Gentrification," p. 55.

27. Urry, *The Tourist Gaze*, p. 120.

28. Edward M. Bruner, "The Transformation of Self in Tourism," *Annals of Tourism Research* 18 (1991): 238–50.

29. Jean-Paul Sartre, *Being and Nothingness*, Hazel E. Barnes, trans. (New York: Philosophical Library, 1956).

30. Lynn Stephen, *Zapotec Women* (Austin: University of Texas Press, 1991), p. 17.

31. Dean MacCannell, "Reconstructed Ethnicity: Tourism and Cultural Identity in Third World Communities," *Annals of Tourism Research* 11, no. 3 (1984): 375–91. This list of types or forms of ethnicity among natives subsumes and further differentiates what MacCannell calls reconstructed ethnicity, which he defines as "the maintenance and preservation of ethnic forms for the entertainment of ethnically different others" (p. 385). Ethnic reconstruction in this sense is only one aspect of a multidimensional response to the expanding tourism economy. MacCannell's suggestion that ethnic reconstruction leads to cultural stagnation and death seems simplistic and does not describe what is happening in Taos. Although tourism does foster a frozen, nostalgic image of the timeless or authentic Indian or Hispano culture, the constant remaking of ethnic symbols and identity by individuals operating within these ossified parameters is fluid, opportunistic, and innovative.

32. Bruner, "Transformation of Self," p. 242.

33. Sylvia Rodríguez, "Land, Water, and Ethnic Identity in Taos," in *Land, Water, and Culture*, C. Briggs and J. Van Ness, eds. (Albuquerque: University of New Mexico Press, 1987), pp. 313–403; Sylvia Rodríguez, "Art, Tourism, and Race Relations in Taos: Toward a Sociology of the Art Colony," *Journal of Anthropological Research* 45, no. 1 (1990): 77-99; and Sylvia Rodríguez, "Ethnic Reconstruction in Contemporary Taos," *Journal of the Southwest* 32, no. 4 (1990): 541–55.

34. I am grateful to José Limón for suggesting the term *surface politics* to refer to the level of ethnic conservationist activity discussed here. As indicated, the *deep politics* of individual subjectivity will be taken up elsewhere.

35. Urry, *The Tourist Gaze*, p. 112.

36. Ibid., p. 114.

37. The *acequia* system involves a colonial-era network of hand-dug ditches used to irrigate all privately owned plots of farmland in any given land grant or offshoot community. Their contemporary maintenance and operation are supervised by elected local commissioners and a *mayordomo*, or ditch boss. As a long-standing public works system, the *acequias* constitute both the material and organizational basis for the traditional, if increasingly superseded, Mexicano agro-pastoral subsistence economy. The ownership and exercise of inherited surface-water rights is one of the key institutions by which Hispanos remain attached to their land base.

38. See Rodríguez, "Land, Water, and Ethnic Identity."

39. John Nichols, *If Mountains Die* (New York: Alfred A. Knopf, 1979).

KARL DOERRY

The American West: Conventions and Inventions in Art and Literature

WHEN CZECH-BORN FILM DIRECTOR Milos Forman won the Oscar for best film—*Amadeus*—in 1984, he was asked in an interview whether he did not find it difficult to work in the popular media of a foreign culture. His reply was that everybody really has two homelands: one, where his mother tongue is spoken; the other, America. When I was growing up in Germany in the 1950s, we all read a very popular book, *Traumland Amerika* (*Dreamland America*), a travelogue of a journey through different regions of the United States. All of these regions were admired for their exotic vastness and grandeur so painfully lacking in postwar Europe.

Both of these anecdotes are examples of a long-standing tradition—on both sides of the Atlantic and perhaps all over the world—of treating America (and for all practical purposes that means the United States) as a genuinely *New* World. In other words, a conceptual alternative to the Old World instead of just an extension or duplication of the known world. At the same time it is clearly a region of the mind, a place where one can feel at home without ever having been there physically.

In his provocative book *The Invention of America*, Edmundo O'Gorman has shown how this intellectual tradition can be traced back to Columbus and other sixteenth-century explorers and indeed to earlier myths like that of Atlantis and the paradise stories common to many cultures. The discovery of the New World simply provided a concrete locale upon which all these Utopian dreams could be projected.

But a Utopian vision and a concrete locale must inevitably collide. In Columbus's first account of his discovery, his famous letter to the Spanish court, this tension was evident. The pervasive paradise imagery—friendly, naked, childlike natives welcoming the Spaniards to their garden-like island with a balmy climate, abundant fruit, and fresh water—was undercut by dark suggestions of cannibalism, licentiousness, and general savagery. From the beginning, the image of the New World has therefore been characterized by the tension between a dream, a set of expectations, and the jarring observations that clash with this dream. This tension gives rise to ever-renewed attempts to reconcile these contradictions: to preserve, in the face of facts, a dreamland somewhere in "the West." When Columbus landed in the Caribbean he had reached the West of his day. When it fell short of perfection, his successors pushed on, westward, to the Seven Cities of Cíbola or to El Dorado, a Utopia of immense riches but, just as importantly, without greed—a place where you could eat your cake without pangs of conscience.

That tradition continues to this very day, when the West has more specifically become the Southwest. This is true, however, only in the sense that the images and iconography associated with it are based on the prominent features of the southwestern landscape—the open spaces of the sparsely populated plains, the spectacular rock formations, and the bright, clear, sunny skies. But one must not forget that it is, for all its resemblance to actual landscapes, an imagined, mythical land, invented as an emblem for dreams and fears important to contemporary culture. In this sense the Southwest is not a particular geographical region. Instead, it is subsumed within the broader conceptions and idealizations of the West, conceptions that are often the products of yearnings from outside the region.

When the facts of life finally catch up with Huck Finn, in the form of the widow Douglas and the threat of schooling, haircuts, and clean clothes, he "lights out for the territories" to preserve the dream of interracial harmony and idyllic drifting that he lived for a brief time on the Mississippi. Mark Twain's closing of *The Adventures of Huckleberry Finn* strikes us as "right," or "classic," because it is a perfect example of what the typical American protagonist is forced to do at the end of the story. Huck's departure is the equivalent of the clichéd Western hero riding off into the sunset. For civilization with its compromises and constraints leaves no room for a life of personal freedom and integrity, no room for the American dream, and the individual has almost no choice but to move on.

If this motif is a cliché to twentieth-century audiences, it was no less familiar to Mark Twain's generation. Natty Bumppo of James Fenimore Cooper's *Leatherstocking Tales* had already familiarized Americans with tales of the conflict between nature and civilization. But what is really remarkable is that this motif is not restricted to American audiences but works equally well for readers who have no direct knowledge of American society.

Between 1827 and 1844 the German-American writer Karl Postl (1793–1864), publishing under the pseudonym Charles Sealsfield, completed a substantial number of works. Some were originally in English and some in German, the latter soon translated into English. In America he was popular enough for Longfellow to mention an evening of reading aloud "our beloved Sealsfield." He had come to the New World as a refugee, hunted by the secret police of Habsburg Austria, after he abandoned his post as secretary in a religious order in 1823. His first publications were two companion volumes: a kind of travelogue-guidebook to the United States, published in 1827; and an exposé about Austria, *Austria as It Is*, published in 1828 and immediately banned in Austria and other German principalities.

By itself the volume on the United States seems factual and harmless enough, but a comparison to its companion volume shows that the New World was portrayed as in every way the positive alternative to the Old World. In the United States the narrator travels freely through a garden-like country of productive farms, whose inhabitants may lack a refined education but act with a natural dignity born of their independence and self-sufficiency. Austria, by contrast, is presented as a country of intrigue, repression, and corruption. While the volume on the United States is dominated by descriptions of pastoral landscapes, the volume on Austria dismisses "the country between Frankfort and Leipsic" as of "little interest." Austria is portrayed as focusing on fashionable society, a society that is seen as exhausted and corrupt and therefore doomed by history. Sealsfield observed that "the tide runs in Vienna towards gross sensuality in the people; abject obedience in the public officers; gloom or dissoluteness among the high nobility; and towards the most complete despotism in the Government, which grasps with the iron claw of its emblem—the double eagle—the whole empire and keeps it in its baneful embraces."[1] Where the reader should look instead is made clear by the author's rendition of world history. Ancient civilizations, he contends,

> rose in the beautiful plains of Euphrates, Tigris, Araxes, and Ganges. They are now a desert. It moved towards the borders of the Mediterranean,—and Lydia and Ephesias shone forth. Their glory is gone too, to make place for the bright star of beautiful Greece, whose splendor sank with the walls of Corinth, and imperial Rome took the command of the world. She is now only extant in the records of history, and Europe's hope rests on the proud Rock of Albion. [An obvious bow toward his British publishers and readers.] But the tide runs

> toward America and perhaps before two centuries . . . the genius of Europe . . . will have alighted on the mighty Mississippi.[2]

Sealsfield thus sees a parallel between his own flight west, across the Atlantic, and the movement of culture from east to west, across the Atlantic. He projects his hopes for the political future of Europe, especially that of Austria and Germany, onto this New World. When his six-volume work, *Life in the New World; or, Sketches of American Society,* appeared in 1844 he added this dedication to the translation:

> To the German nation
> Roused to the consciousness of its power and dignity
> These pictures of the
> Domestic and Public Life of
> Free Citizens of a Free State
> Destined to Historical Greatness
> are respectfully
> dedicated as a Mirror for Self-Examination
> by the Author[3]

The most striking character in these sketches is Nathan, a squatter and "regulator" (a kind of unofficial judge and sheriff), who has established a small community in the Louisiana wilderness. His settlement thrives, but when official civilization arrives and Nathan and his community are found to be without legal title, they have to move west, where they found a settlement some one hundred miles beyond San Antonio, Texas. The last volume is subtitled *The First American in Texas*, a recognition of the Southwest as a region for social renewal and hope.

The subsequent development of Texas is the basis for Sealsfield's most successful work, *The Cabinbook*, a fictionalized account of Texas's struggle for independence. The book's climax is the Battle of San Jacinto in 1836. Its publication in 1841 thus gave it an historical immediacy, while its success also testifies to the great interest that the political developments in Texas had for the partisan left of Europe on the eve of the 1848 revolutions. What makes the novel so interesting and revealing in our context is that it combined typically western and southwestern imagery and scenery with the explicitly political themes that interested Sealsfield.

The "cabin" of the book's title refers to the dwelling of a former sea captain. It was a dwelling shaped like a sailing ship's cabin but also like a log cabin, tying together the image of the ocean crossed by European immigrants and of the western plain they are about to conquer. In this cabin, various narrators tell the interrelated stories that form the novel. The main narrator is a Colonel Morse, who is later revealed to have been a decisive participant at the Battle of San Jacinto.

He begins by relating his initiation to Texas. Lured from Maryland by a fraudulent contract to buy ten thousand acres of Texas land, he arrives at Galveston and is struck by the difficulty of telling land from ocean. "The most experienced sailors have trouble here, for since the land barely rises from the ocean, it disappears behind even the smallest swell; yes, the swaying green of the prairie grasses resembles the waves of the equally green coastal water. . . . There was no coast, no land, at least we could not tell one from the other."[4] As they sail up the Río Bravo, he continues to marvel at the "grass ocean" around him dotted with clumps of trees, which the locals call "islands." The crossing of the Texas prairie thus is portrayed as a direct extension of the ocean crossings preceding the settling of the New World. This crossing is accompanied by the same "sea changes" experienced by the first settlers.

The newcomers to Texas, including not a few hard-boiled ruffians, fall silent in the face of this natural grandeur. "Everything so still, solemn, and majestic! . . . so fresh, so pure, as if recently emerged from the hand of the eternal master craftsman. No trace of the sinful hand of man: God's pure, unsullied creation."[5]

But very quickly Morse discovers that the Southwest is no easy paradise. Pursuing a runaway horse, he loses his way in this "meadow ocean." After wandering aimlessly for several days, he faints from exhaustion and hallucinates about being in the underworld. He is then found and revived by a demonic character, a murderer who hides out in the prairie but is constantly pursued by the ghosts of his victims. This representative of evil at first seems totally out of place in the paradise prairie; yet he not only saves Morse's life but eventually helps secure the independence of the state of Texas. His heroic self-sacrifice assures the defeat of the Mexican forces in the decisive battle.

Immersing himself in this ocean-like prairie, then, is like a baptism—a death and rebirth. The greenhorn Easterner, who came to Texas in search of easy riches, is transformed into a politically mature Westerner. He is now a man who understands and is in tune with the divine plan for the progress of civilization, a plan in which even criminals play a useful part. As one of Morse's western mentors explains,

> In the prairie you see things in a different light than in your cities. For your cities are created by humans and polluted by their breath, while the prairie is created by God and his breath. And your sight clouded by city fumes is cleared by this pure breath most wonderfully. It's a beautiful thing, this enlightenment, when you see to the bottom of truth, seeing how the great statesman up there operates employing for his most beautiful, magnificent works the most desperate individuals, even veritable devils.[6]

Sealsfield thus presents the West as a Utopia in which the contradictions of his time are reconciled in a manner not possible either in Europe or in the urban East, which has already become too Europeanized. In this Southwest people can live in a free state without the anarchy so recently exemplified by the French Revolution. In the New World, such anarchy is shown to serve the establishment of democratic freedoms in the long run. Like Morse, people can become wealthy without being greedy. As Texas moves toward "happiness" in joining the Union, Morse finds personal happiness in his own union with the daughter of his host. The political paradise of Texas is duplicated and reflected by the "paradise of love," as the book's concluding chapter is entitled.

This equation of the New World, and in particular its West and Southwest, with paradise had become enough of a cliché in the mid-nineteenth century for Charles Dickens to exploit it for satire in his *American Notebooks* and in *Martin Chuzzlewit*. In the latter, he sends his protagonist off to the frontier settlement of Eden, which turns out to be everything but paradisiacal. But his effort at debunking this ideal, as well as the attempts of many other writers, did little to diminish it. For any criticism of America could (and still can) be answered by the argument that the "real" and better America is "out there," somewhere to the West.

This is exemplified by one of Sealsfield's German successors, Friedrich Gerstäcker, who lived from 1816 to 1872. One generation after Sealsfield, he produced around one hundred fifty volumes of travel and adventure books, many of them about America. Although his books contain many negative images of the New World, these are, as in Sealsfield, confined to the corrupt cities of the East, which are dismissed as somehow not the real America. "The East was of no interest to him," Gerstäcker writes of one of his protagonists. ". . . He would only become acquainted with the less civilized parts; he sought that America which he had pictured to himself and which he could not find in Cincinnati or any other city where culture had progressed."[7]

"He sought that America which he had pictured to himself" is a revealing phrase—an America, in other words, of his dreams. Sealsfield pictured for his readers a democratic union of states, a dream so common to the middle-class intellectuals of his society. He projected that dream upon Texas and the West of the New World. Gerstäcker, writing after that particular dream had been shattered with the suppression of the 1848 revolutions, projected onto the West a different dream, that of *individual* instead of *political* freedom. While Sealsfield saw the western paradise turn the individual into a better citizen, Gerstäcker idolized the frontiersman who thrives by himself in the wilderness. His works are full of rhapsodic descriptions of a wilderness paradise:

> What a wonderful interplay of color there is in the foliage . . . with that mighty, dark tree as a focal point, from which beams actually shoot out like rays in every direction!—And those iridescent festoons which are twined around the oak with gold and purple leaves . . . and the masses of dark blue grapes suspended from them—oh how beautiful, how wonderfully lovely is this land.[8]

But this paradise generates not political systems but heroic individuals like Jack Owen, in the emigrant saga *To America:*

> [He]. . . was a powerful, manly figure. His hair was curly, his eyes blue and the expression of his face was decidedly honest and straightforward . . . in a word, a superb prototype of that mighty steel-hardened race of individuals who traverse the western primeval forest of the Union, first as hunters, and then with their daring settle it with their "improvements" . . . and armed solely with rifle and axe create a home for themselves in the shadow of the dense wilderness.[9]

It is easy to recognize in the American "prototype" a Natty Bumppo, Davy Crockett, Jedediah Smith, and other assorted western heroes. But Jack Owen not only has some distinctly Teutonic features, he was also invented by Gerstäcker as a direct positive alternative to his German counterpart. "In vain will the immigrant seek in the American farmer for a trace of that coarse, clumsy behavior which distinguishes our farm people. . . . The American farmer recognizes no superior group and the feeling of independence which is his gives him that unconstrained I should like to call it genteel bearing which in our circles reveals the man of the world."[10] Again we see a writer and his readers look to the western frontier as a place where dreams can come true—in this case, a place where a farmer can become "genteel" and "a man of the world." In a word, an aristocrat.

Superficially, it may seem paradoxical to glorify the home of modern democracy for giving rise to aristocrats. But the readers for whom these books were written, the rising middle class, had long aspired to aristocratic amenities like coaches, estates, plantations, and elegant balls, as well as refined speech and a code of honor. As these luxuries could not be found very frequently in the nineteenth-century West and Southwest, writers frequently projected them onto that original American, the Indian.

There is no lack of disparaging depictions of Native Americans. Yet the notion that they represent a purer, better American persists in American writing from the accounts of Columbus, or from the story of the Pilgrims' first Thanksgiving and Cooper's Unkas and Chinchagook, to Ken Kesey's Chief Bromden in *One Flew over the Cuckoo's Nest* and Tony Hillerman's Navajo detectives.

Although these positive portraits share much with the broader tradition of the "noble savage," the natives of the American West are always a good deal nobler than other primitive races. South Sea islanders, such as Gauguin's Tahitian or Melville's Polynesians, are typically attractive but immature children, and blacks are usually portrayed as overly emotional and incapable of serious thought. In contrast, Indians are likely to be endowed with not only an ability for philosophizing but also with a capacity for solemn rhetoric. The image of blacks in nineteenth-century writing seems to preclude the possibility that they might speak correctly, let alone memorably. Indians, on the other hand—from Chief Joseph to Black Elk to Thomas Berger's Old Lodge Skins in *Little Big Man*—have long been readily accepted as great rhetoricians.

It defies logic to assume that Indians had a more powerful command of language than blacks, particularly after emancipation, when the tradition of black preaching was well established. So this convention of the innate rhetorical gift of Indians is clearly an invention. It implies that the Indian is a better, "truer" American, paradoxically because he has a deep kinship to that ancient European tradition from which American democracy took its clues: that the Indian is, at heart, a Roman.

One need only look at Federal architecture, with its predominance of columns and Greco-Roman classical lines, to realize how much this new nation, with a Senate and consul-like president, looked to the Roman republic as a model. It was therefore only natural to claim Chief Joseph as an American Cicero, and the American artists of the nineteenth century

Fig. 1. Charles Bird King's *Young Omahaw, War Eagle, Little Missouri, and Pawnees* (oil on canvas, 1821) draws upon Roman imaging in its depiction of Native Americans. (Reproduced with permission, gift of Miss Helen Barlow. National Museum of American Art, Smithsonian Institution.)

were eager to portray Indians as noble Romans in feather headdresses and to diminish their non-European facial features. When a Pawnee tribal delegation visited Washington in 1821, one observer described them: "All of them were men of large stature, very muscular, having fine open countenances, with the real noble Roman nose, dignified in their manners and peaceful and quiet in their habits."[11] Members of this delegation were painted by Charles Bird King in a multiple portrait that shows the Pawnees as more Roman than Indian. Their robes are draped like togas over their naked shoulders, exposing a medal as it might have been worn by Caesar Augustus, and their facial features seem to be borrowed from Roman statuary. Most of the 143 portraits of Indians that King painted between 1821 and 1842 demonstrated these same qualities of Indians as calmly heroic Romans (fig. 1).

Fig. 2. George Catlin's *Clermont, First Chief of the Tribe* (oil on canvas, 1834) is painted in the pastoral tradition. Conventional European poses and facial features helped Native Americans appear more familiar. (Reproduced with permission, gift of Mrs. Joseph Harrison, Jr. National Museum of American Art, Smithsonian Institution.)

If King stressed the motif of the heroic Roman, George Catlin focused on the pastoral tradition. His portraits of *Clermont, First Chief of the Tribe* (Osage) and of Clermont's wife (both also enshrined in the National Museum of American Art) show the couple sitting before a background of soothing pastel pinks and blues, looking at the viewer calmly and without threat (figs. 2 and 3). Both are posed in a conventional way, and their faces have regular European features. Clermont's club is cradled in his arms in a most un-warlike manner, much like the child on his wife's lap. He wears a peace medal, sign of his reconciliation with the white man, and his wife in her flowing robes suggests a Roman matron with her child—perhaps, with her blue cloak, even a Madonna and child. In any case, these are soothingly familiar figures for the viewer, even models, and certainly not savages.

A third example of this Roman-Indian motif is Ferdinand Pettrich's sculpture *The Dying Tecumseh* (1856). Executed in marble, the life-size statue seems to belong on the sarcophagus of a Roman field marshal (fig. 4). Completed a generation after Catlin, the sculpture exemplifies an

Fig. 3. George Catlin's *Wah-chee-te, Wife of Clermont, and Child* (oil on canvas, 1834) suggests a Roman matron and child, perhaps even Madonna and child, helping to Europeanize Native Americans. (Reproduced with permission, gift of Mrs. Joseph Harrison, Jr. National Museum of American Art, Smithsonian Institution.)

additional and increasingly common aspect of the idealized portrait of the Indian: the emphasis on the "vanishing American." Tecumseh may resemble a noble Roman, but like Rome he must make room for the new civilization. His death, the work implies, may be regrettable, even tragic, but is to be accepted without remorse as part of the progress of history.

It may be useful to note that these writers and artists, portraying such western and southwestern motifs, were strangers and newcomers to their regions. Sealsfield and Gerstäcker were emigrants from Europe. Catlin, who did travel in the West, was born and lived most of his life in Pennsylvania and the East. King was from Rhode Island and trained as a painter in New York and Great Britain. Pettrich was born in Germany and studied sculpture in Dresden and Rome before moving to the United States at the age of thirty-seven. Albert Bierstadt and Thomas Moran, both European-born, have become the archetypical painters of sublime western landscapes. And German-born and -trained Emmanuel Leutze not only produced the ultimate patriotic American painting in *Washington Crossing the Delaware* (1851) but also the supreme celebration of western expansion in *Westward*

Fig. 4. *The Dying Tecumseh*, a marble sculpture carved by Frederick Augustus Ferdinand Pettrich in 1856, seems to belong on the sarcophagus of a Roman field marshal and implies a progressive view of history: the death of one civilization, in this case Native American, leads to the rise of another. (Reproduced with permission. National Museum of American Art, Smithsonian Institution.)

the Course of Empire Takes Its Way (1862), the monumental 20 ft. x 30 ft. painting in the United States Capitol.

The fact that the image of the West was shaped largely by Easterners is, of course, no surprise, because most Westerners in the early nineteenth century had neither the leisure nor the inclination, nor much of a market, for painting or literature. But the fact remains that the West has always been an artistic invention of Easterners, a reality that in no way changed when the West became more hospitable to artists around the beginning of the twentieth century.

Becoming more hospitable meant, of course, that the Old West had passed, and the painters or writers who came West set themselves the task, quite consciously, to preserve what they thought this West had been or should have been. "We fellows who are doing the 'Old America' which is so fast passing," wrote Frederic Remington to fellow western painter Carl Runguis, "will have an audiance [*sic*] in posterity whether we do at present or not."[12] Doing, redoing, even creating the Old America was indeed the agenda of artists like Remington or a writer like Owen Wister, and very much in tune with their friend and fellow Easterner Theodore Roosevelt. But by doing the *old* America, they also saw this creation very much in contrast and opposition to their *contemporary* America. They viewed the Old West with nostalgia and projected onto it qualities they found painfully absent in their own time.

1993 was the centennial of Frederick Jackson Turner's famous thesis that the existence of the frontier, of open land in the West, was the decisive factor in shaping the culture of the New World. In 1893 that frontier had just been closed, and Turner's thesis itself implies the end of one era and the beginning of a new, uncertain one. The work of Remington and Wister reflects this uncertainty. They and their fellow Easterners saw themselves in a world of rising capitalism and urbanization, besieged by a tide of immigrants. In response they invented an Old West where these tensions are either absent altogether or at least under control, and the familiar conventions of the classical Western can be seen as direct responses to these threats.

Although the topography of the United States west of the Mississippi varies greatly, the landscape of the Western never changes and is almost exclusively restricted to southwestern scenery. Dominated by wide open spaces with wide, clear vistas, it is not so much a geographical as a morally symbolic landscape. Here clarity of vision is not just physical. Just as the dust of a rider can be seen from miles away, moral distinctions are clear at first sight. This West is not a place of moral ambiguities: the villain is easily recognized in the first scene. He is evil by nature, cannot be rehabilitated by good advice or punishment, and therefore can be eliminated by violence without remorse. This is in sharp contrast to the complexity of life in the urban East, the daily reality of writers like Owen Wister and artists like Remington and of their audiences. They viewed themselves as surrounded by "robber barons" who were also praised as philanthropists; they saw their government send troops to liberate Cuba but allow those troops to be poisoned by spoiled food supplied by corrupt contractors at huge profits; and they felt themselves powerless to control their lives and the economic threats around them. They therefore found it irresistible to identify with the independent Western hero who is both nobler and more powerful than the dark forces around him.

Thus, the Westerns offer escape to a precapitalist sanctuary for an audience who believes its political and economic independence to be sorely threatened. Although we commonly speak of cowboy stories, movies, or art, Westerns deal only very peripherally with a cowboy's work and other economic aspects like the cattle market, the price of commodities, or interest rates. Even Owen Wister's Virginian, a working cowboy and foreman, is rarely seen at work. He distinguishes himself by practical jokes, as a genteel suitor, as a great storyteller, and finally as a superb gunman. But at no time does he or any other fictional cowboy ever have to worry about unemployment or money.

This is true even of the typical Western villain. Wister's antagonist, Trampas, competes for power and prestige but not for economic advantage, for in the fictional West it is a firm rule that money doesn't matter. Even when stagecoaches or banks are robbed or cattle is rustled, the moral offense is always more important than the economic damage.

But in spite or perhaps because of the hero's disdain for riches, they often seem to fall into his lap. In this West, it seems, one gets rich without compromising one's values for the sake of economic gains. Thus Wister's Virginian ends up as a prospective Wyoming coal magnate without really trying. While other Western heroes may not achieve quite that level of wealth, they never seem to worry about making a living. This principle is demonstrated very clearly by Zane Grey's 1913 novel, *Desert Gold.*

The protagonist from the East has failed his family's expectations for success in business and is banished to Arizona. "So Dick bade goodbye to fine suits of clothes and linen with a feeling that as he had said farewell to an idle and useless past, it was just as well not to have any old luxuries as reminders." His host in Arizona confirms this but also amends: "Money's the last thing we think of out here. All the same, Gale, if you stick you'll be rich."[13] Of course he does "stick" and is rewarded by "desert gold"—quite literally when he discovers a gold mine, but also figuratively by winning the hand of his love, by discovering a hidden spring in the desert, and more generally by finding his manhood through a struggle with Mexican bandits as well as with the harsh desert. His father, reconciled at last, congratulates him on his "gold" strike. "But it seemed to Dick himself that his father meant something very different from love and fortune in his allusion to desert gold."[14] Underneath the harsh surface of the Southwest, Zane Grey implies, lie material and spiritual riches that fall to those who persist.

The Southwest, here and elsewhere, solves the problems of the East. In Zane Grey's novel these problems are fairly trivial and shallow, essentially the personal problems of the protagonist. Wister, on the other hand, is much more conscious of the tension between East and West embodied in the classical Western.

The most central chapter in *The Virginian* has little relevance to the plot. Titled "Quality and Equality," it starts with the Virginian's confession that a Russian novel lent to him by a young woman named Molly had nearly moved him to tears. The title is never mentioned, but it is clear that the book in question is Turgenev's *Fathers and Sons*, in itself a remarkable indication of how well-educated a reader Wister had in mind for his Western. The Virginian is touched by this novel because he feels a kinship with Turgenev's protagonist, who knows himself to be an exceptional individual. He even compares himself to Napoleon but also finds himself in circumstances that stifle his genius. Like him, the Virginian "felt himself to be a giant whom life had made broad gauge, and denied opportunity".[15] This leads to the chapter's central discussion of quality and equality. Molly, the Eastern schoolteacher, tries to uphold the conventional position that "all men are born equal" but is forced to admit that "equality is a great big bluff." The Virginian confronts her with repeated examples of how seemingly equal individuals nevertheless fare very differently in life: "Call your failure luck, or call it laziness, wander around the words, prospect all yu mind to, and ya'll come out the same old trail of inequality. . . . Some holds four aces—and some holds nothing, and some poor fello' gets the aces and no show to play em; but a man has to prove himself my equal before I'll believe him."[16]

If this is a surprising topic of discussion between a cowboy and his sweetheart, the narrator's subsequent peroration is even more surprising in a Western.

> It was through the Declaration of Independence that we Americans acknowledged the eternal inequality of man. For by it we abolished a cut-and-dried aristocracy. We had seen little men artificially held up in high places, and great men artificially held down in low places, and our own justice-loving hearts abhorred this violence to human nature. Therefore, we decreed that every man should thenceforth have equal liberty to find his own level. By this very decree we acknowledged and gave freedom to true aristocracy, saying, "Let the best man win, whoever he is." Let the best man win! That is America's word. That is true democracy. And true democracy and true aristocracy are one and the same thing. If anybody cannot see this, so much the worse for his eyesight.[17]

Though we may find such editorializing somewhat incongruous in a Western, the passage does draw attention to the fact that topical political and social issues underlie his Western. Although they are rarely articulated as explicitly as here, they have remained central to the genre. Its Old West is a place where the unnatural inequalities of an artificial aristocracy have been abolished and where the unnatural equality of organized democracy has not yet been established. For a brief interlude "true democracy," the true America, is possible. Once again the West is an emblem for the "real America," and its attractions are a measure of how far the audience's everyday life falls short of this ideal.

It is a measure of a writer's skill to persuade his readers of the validity of his invention, and his persuasiveness may in turn be a function of his own belief in it. Two important ways to achieve such persuasiveness are richness in accurate details and repetition.

Western art, whether verbal or representational, prides itself on its authenticity of detail. Many of our best-known western artists (such as Frederic Remington) were also avid collectors of western artifacts, did field or museum studies for their works, and frequently criticized fellow artists who got details wrong. They regularly claimed that they were preserving the historical record of a vanishing era. It is, of course, a very partial and therefore a falsified or "invented" record—showing, for instance, a West that is curiously untouched by economic and racial conflicts in the rest of the nation. Even though many liberated slaves found work as cowboys, blacks do not exist in Westerns. Though Wister's Virginian hints that he fought in the Civil War, its issues are never mentioned. The passion for accuracy professed by artists from Remington and Russell to present-day Hollywood studios thus is highly selective and merely serves to give their fiction the appearance of authenticity.

The other method of convincing readers, and the authors themselves, that the "truth" of the West is portrayed is use of almost compulsive repetition. Each new showdown on Main Street, barroom brawl, or break-neck chase confirms all past and future examples of these conventions and establishes the sense that these adrenalin rushes were not only part of everyday life in the West but also glimpses of an eternal pattern. Invoking the same incidents and the same set of characters with minor variations over and over again gives the Western the hypnotic quality of a ritual, with its claim of access to a transcendent and archetypal reality. The horseman, the cowpuncher, Owen Wister claims in the foreword to *The Virginian*, "will be here among us always, invisible" as "his wild kind has been among us always, since the beginning."[18]

But all too often the hypnotist is the first to become resistant to his own spell. The Western arose in response to the closing of the frontier, and one of its conventions has always been the melancholy—the consciousness of time passing. Wister's claim to the timelessness of the horseman clashes ironically with the close of the novel: the West has become like the East, run by corrupt politicians, and the Virginian as coal baron seems to be despoiling the same land that made him possible. His fight against Trampas and his gang had been a last stand. Though victorious in that battle, he has lost the war; thieves, the politicians, and Eastern money men take over the pristine West.

This motif of "the last stand" is part of the Western genre from the beginning, repeated in Western after Western, with particular clarity in "late" specimens of the genre. Examples are *The Gunfighter* with Gregory Peck or *The Shootist* with John Wayne, where the weary hero appears almost glad to be relieved of his life and the obligation to uphold a code of conduct that has become irrelevant. But even if the hero survives and rides off into the sunset, or the dawn of a new married life, as Gary Cooper does at the end of *High Noon* (a change from the story on which the film is based, in which he dies of the wounds suffered in the showdown), he is exiled from the town that he has just made safe for democratic institutions.

The Old West and the values it is made to represent are therefore always seen as under siege by hostile forces. "Last stand" situations abound. "Custer's Last Stand," the best-known of many, was not only endlessly depicted in popular illustrations but was a standard part of Wild West shows such as Buffalo Bill's. But Remington's *A Dash for the Timber* (1889), *The Last Stand* (1890), *Rounded Up* (1890), or *The Intruders* (1910); Schreyvogel's *Defending the Stockade* (1905); Charles Russell's *Caught in the Circle* (1903); and Henry Forny's *Rounded-Up by God* (1906) are just some examples of how all-pervasive this motif was in western art around the turn of the century. Indeed, volume four of Theodore Roosevelt's *The Winning of the West* featured yet another of Remington's last-stand paintings, *Fight for the Waterhole* (1903), as a frontispiece in the 1904 edition. A large representative painting (27 in. x 40 in.), it is remarkable for the subtlety with which it communicates its sense of doom (fig. 5). The five defenders besieged by indistinct opponents, perhaps Indians, have held their own so far, but time is clearly running out for them. The spent bullet casings scattered around them suggest that their ammunition may be running low and that the fight has gone on for some time. Indeed, the round

Fig. 5. Frederic Remington's *Fight for the Waterhole* (oil on canvas, 1903) conveys a sense of doom for the particular men fighting an unseen enemy and, by extension, implies a vanishing way of life for those outnumbered by progress. (Gift of Miss Ima Hogg, the Hogg Brothers Collection, Museum of Fine Arts, Houston.)

water hole with the cowboys arranged around its rim suggests a clock face. The shadows are engulfing the water hole, which may become a grave; the sand already seems to be swallowing up the body of one of the cowboys in the background. They may be courageous, competent, even heroic. But they are doomed, nevertheless, to fall to the onslaught of distant dangers or, should they prevail in this fight, to the onslaught of time.

It is open to speculation how conscious Remington and his contemporaries were of the implications of their "last-stand" tableaus. What is not in doubt is that a siege mentality, the feeling that the soul of the United States was threatened, was very widespread around the turn of the century and that these artists shared that feeling and reflected it in their works. We must remember that this was also the time of widespread and violent labor unrest, strikes, and riots. Battles with police, often mounted, made it easy to see parallels to frontier violence. When Owen Wister in 1911 rededicated the second edition of *The Virginian* to Teddy Roosevelt, he praised him for saving America from its "many enemies both in Wall Street and in the Labor Unions,"[19] just as a Western hero saves the community from its multitude of enemies. Remington proclaimed himself personally ready to deal with un-American threats in the fashion of the frontier. "You can't glorify a Jew—coin-loving 'puds'—nasty humans," he wrote in a letter. "I've got some Winchesters and when the massacring begins . . . I can get my share of 'em and what's more I will. . . . Jews—inguns [*sic*]—chinamen—Italians—Huns, the rubish [*sic*] of the earth I hate."[20] Remington and his contemporaries invented the West as a sanctuary, a place where such "rubish" was either absent or reliably controlled.

It is surely no accident that the Western experienced a renaissance after World War II, when the country again felt its values threatened by the postwar economic boom, the external threat of the Cold War, and the internal challenge to democratic American values posed by McCarthyism. In what often has been called the first big political television show, the American public watched, often in between Westerns, a drama in which people were accused of having violated the Western's code of openness and frankness by committing deception, conspiracy, and treachery—thus seeming like the bad guys. At the same time many of these "witnesses" appeared to remain faithful to their own internal code of conduct and did not denounce their friends and companions, even against the most intense community pressure—surely a mark of a good guy. To conclude the confusion, the inquisitor McCarthy, sneering, bullying, and always seeming to need a shave, looked every bit like a Western bad guy. No wonder audiences preferred the clarity of the Westerns that dominated much of the rest of television programming.

Fred Zinneman's *High Noon* has always been considered a conscious response to McCarthyism. But this interpretation of the film as a direct allegory of the struggle against McCarthyism obscures all other meanings of the film. Indeed it would not be too difficult to reverse this interpretation: the villain could just as well be taken to stand for communism threatening to take over but defeated by the undaunted American hero doing "what a man has to do."

A more broadly based interpretation is to see this Western, together with innumerable other examples of the postwar decades, as appealing to audiences by offering an alternative to their morally ambiguous and problematic present. It is a West in which villains are not only easy to recognize but also so incorrigible that there is no alternative to killing them. In this way, these Westerns helped to reconcile the American public to the use of violence in World War II and Korea by confirming the righteousness of such actions. The compulsiveness with which Westerns were consumed by the audiences of the 1950s, as well as the moral ironies introduced by some Westerns late in this era, strongly suggest a moral uneasiness that constantly needed to be calmed.

The violence of these Westerns is usually committed against the representatives of barbarism in order to make room for "civilization." But as we have seen, that civilization is associated with the East and depicted as inferior. If the struggle and sacrifice of the hero only serve to make the West safe for con men and money grubbers, the hero becomes at best an ironic or quixotic figure, at worst a clown. Thus Edward Abbey in *The Brave Cowboy* (1958), and its film version, *Lonely Are the Brave* (1961), pitches a protagonist who takes the Western conventions seriously against a modern world of jet planes, helicopters, and draft boards. He fights off the representatives of twentieth-century corruption for a while, even bringing down a helicopter with a lucky shot from his saddle gun. But in the end he dies unheroically, run over by a tractor-trailer loaded with toilets.

Larry McMurtry has called Abbey the Thoreau of the American West, and Abbey himself consciously compared himself to his fellow Easterner when he titled one of his last books *Down the River with Henry David Thoreau*. Like Thoreau, Abbey continuously spoke out in defense of the West as the last stronghold of "wilderness," a wilderness in environment and spirit that he praised as the essence of America. But the most sustained literary effort to reexamine and reshape the popular image of the Old West created by the Western tradition may well be Thomas Berger's 1964 novel, *Little Big Man*.

Berger pays homage to all western and southwestern conventions by inverting them. The locales of his novel, from Santa Fe to Montana, are right; the time period from the 1860s to 1876 is right; and so are incidents and characters. These include Indian attacks on wagon trains and stagecoaches, Colonel Chivington and the Sand Creek massacre, and Custer at the Washita and the Little Big Horn, not to mention cameo appearances by Wild Bill Hickok, Wyatt Earp, and Calamity Jane. But all of these conventions are inverted. The protagonist is a diminutive, confused wanderer between cultures; the supposed heroes of the West are sociopaths and psychopaths; and the Indians appear civilized while the cavalry seems barbarous. The reader learns all this by participating in the education of Berger's protagonist Jack Crabb, an ironic J. C. whose truth about the West may free Americans of the misconceptions about the past that have misguided them in the present.

Jack Crabb's—and the reader's—education can best be seen in the changing image of his Cheyenne mentor, Old Lodge Skins. In their first encounter, Old Lodge Skins seems to confirm the clichéd image of the drunken, illiterate Indian. He presents a comic letter of introduction and falls over instantly upon downing a single drink of whiskey. As we learn more about him, however, he reveals impressive magical powers, becomes a Teiresias-like blind seer, and is thus a credible spokesman to pronounce the novel's concepts of the nature of two conflicting civilizations—the object of the education that this *Bildungsroman* is all about.

The progress of this education is structured by Jack Crabb's alternation between white and Cheyenne society. As he is never fully at home in either, he remains a fresh observer. He is, in effect, the "traveler from abroad" familiar from many Utopian novels. What emerges consistently about white culture is its devotion to appearance and therefore deception, to "talking about how things *should* be rather than as they *was* . . . whereas an Indian has it the other way around."[21]

Nothing in the white world is therefore what it seems to be: the minister's wife is a slut, the famous gunman Wild Bill Hickok a henpecked coward, and the foremost representative of the white world, General Custer, is revealed as a vicious psychopath. Custer leads his troops to their death because his obsession with how things should be prevents him from seeing how dangerous things are. Sometimes Jack Crabb is a victim of these deceptions, as when his business partners cheat him, but as a white man he also participates in them, as when he cheats at cards or disguises himself as a cavalry trooper to get into Custer's presence.

The Indians, on the other hand, are always the victims of deception, except at the Little Big Horn, where they lure the cavalry into a trap and fight from cover. They win because they have adopted the white man's deceptive methods and thus have, in a way, betrayed their culture. Ironically, they win the battle but lose the war of cultures. For in the past their culture has been based on acceptance of reality, including its violence and uncertainty. "If you had to reduce the quality of Cheyenne life to a handy phrase,"[22] Jack Crabb points out, "you might describe it as the constant taking of risks." The white man, by contrast, is shown to strive for stability, permanence, and predictability, the attributes conventionally associated with civilization. What Berger's novel does is to show that the absence of these qualities in Cheyenne culture does not mean no civilization but the presence of a *different*, and in many ways a superior, civilization.

The most radical reversal of convention made by Berger's novel is therefore the reversal of Indians from savages to "Human Beings," the term the Cheyenne apply to themselves. This is a reversal of even the seemingly positive clichéd image of the noble savage, for even a "noble savage" is still a "savage." Berger's Indians are savage. They smell and fornicate, and scalp and mutilate in battle. But all this is seen as part of a coherent life affirming their understanding of reality, which is symbolized by the circles that pervade their existence.

They live in round tepees set up in circles and follow the cyclical migrations of the buffalo herds which, in turn, are determined by the cycles of the seasons. The white man, by contrast, lives in square houses in square blocks and travels on straight trails or builds the straight railroad that cuts through the circle of seasonal migrations on the plains.

These physical manifestations have their equivalents in the way both cultures think. Whites look ahead and behind to define themselves in relation to other men or the rest of creation. Berger's Cheyennes see no reason to get ahead, for there is no "ahead" on a circle. They speak to their ponies or other animals as equals and don't even have a word for "ambition."

Being on a circle the Indians are never disoriented, since they know "where the center of the earth is."[23] Because they see everything as part of the cycle of life they do not see death as a radical disruption to be feared, and every day can therefore be a "a good day to die." The white man, on the other hand, fears death and tries to avoid and deny it as part of his general self-deception. Inevitably, he thus denies life itself. As usual, Old Lodge Skins is the spokesman for this insight. "The Human Beings believe that everything is alive: not only men and animals but also water and earth and stones. . . . But white men believe that everything is dead: stones, earth, animals, and people, even their own people. And if, in spite of that, things persist in trying to live, white men will rub them out."[24]

This seems, at first, like a mere reversal of the convention of Indians as death-dealing savages and white men as preservers of life and civilization. The film version indeed never goes beyond such a reversal. There we see the U.S. cavalry slaughtering women and children and hope for some kind of super-cavalry to ride to the rescue to stop these barbarians. But in the novel, Old Lodge Skins eventually develops a more complex and deeper understanding of the differences. Ironically, Berger makes him recognize Little Big Horn as the *Indians'* last stand:

> It is finished now, because what more can you do to any enemy than beat him. There is no permanent winning or losing when things move, as they should, in a circle. For is not life continuous? And though I shall die, shall I not also continue to live in everything that is? The buffalo eats grass, I eat him, and when I die the earth eats me and sprouts more grass. Therefore nothing is ever lost and each thing is everything forever, though all things move.[25]

And just as the individual is part of this cyclical pattern, the concept of "human being" is not tied to a particular race. "Even if my people must eventually pass from the face of the earth, they will live on in whatever men are fierce and strong. So that when women see a man who is proud, brave and vengeful, even if he has a white face, they will cry: 'That is a Human Being.' "[26]

Thus, for all his debunking of the validity of the conventional images of the Old West, Berger also revitalizes them. He reinvents them with new meanings to embody a distinctly modern and, in a way, "eastern" vision of tribal community values and ecological harmony—a vision much more characteristic of the 1960s than of the 1860s. The makers of the film version went even further when they drew a deliberate parallel between the nineteenth-century Seventh Cavalry massacring Indians at the Washita and the twentieth-century Seventh Cavalry burning villages in Vietnam. Both versions show that the Western is only ostensibly about a very small part of nineteenth-century American history. More importantly, it is always about the present as projected onto an extraordinarily adaptable myth of the past.

For that projection, Berger reaches back to a long-submerged belief that made the original inhabitants of America the embodiment and guardians of the hopes and positive expectations for a genuinely *New* world, a world free of the negatives of the old one. For a while this positive image was overshadowed by the view of Indians as savages, either as a threat to the physical survival of Anglo-Saxon settlers or as symbols of a more generalized non-European "otherness." Only when Indians ceased to be a threat to anyone did they again become available as an emblem for the values that the dominant culture saw slipping away.

In the 1960s we therefore saw a *Return of the Vanishing American*, as Leslie Fiedler called his 1972 book. Though he considered mainly examples from literature, the evidence for his thesis remains plentiful throughout American culture. Beginning in the counterculture of the 1960s, homage to "Indian culture" can now be found in everything from fashion design, Southwest style, to anti-litter billboards and see-the-USA travel ads. These uses of the Indian myth can be complex and profound, like Berger's, or banal, like the tear in the Indian's eye on the anti-litter billboard. But they all evoke values like antimaterialism; a nonhierarchical, community-centered tribal life-style; freedom from schedules, bureaucracies, and social obligations; and, above all, a sense of oneness with the world. There is harmony not only with the physical environment but with an underlying moral stability as well. Clearly these are all attributes of reality sorely missed by contemporary audiences.

One of the most remarkable recent examples of this cultural nostalgia is the extraordinary success of the detective novels of Tony Hillerman. Set in the Southwest, they are truly odd intruders onto the *New York Times* bestseller list, normally reserved for more sensational books. In an unusual mixture, Hillerman joins two sets of seemingly clashing conventions: those of the Western and those of the detective novel. Both traditions arose almost simultaneously in the mid- to late nineteenth century. Thus, they share the same social context as well as certain formal qualities, like the quest motif with a hero battling the forces of evil. But while the Western and its iconography stress openness, clarity, and light, the detective novel features deception, mystery, and darkness. While the Western skies are not cloudy all day, the detective often has to work at night. The hero of a Western can spot his opponent miles away; the detective has to track down his adversary in the confusing labyrinth of the city and identify him among thousands of other men and women who all look alike.

In early detective novels, these difficulties are balanced by the fact that the detective knows himself to be in tune with society. Even if he is not formally a policeman, he delivers the criminal into the hands of the grateful state. That cooperation has become increasingly precarious. As contemporary audiences have grown more skeptical about the moral legitimacy of the state and its agencies, it has become more difficult to create a plausible motivation for the detective's service to a society whose values neither he nor the readers share. Hillerman's Navajo detectives give him a way out of this dilemma. They draw moral strength as well as investigative inspiration from their cultural heritage, which gives them a sense of order and harmony lacking in their Anglo counterparts.

For Joe Leaphorn and Jim Chee, a crime becomes a violation of their Navajo sense of balance and beauty:

> Leaphorn never counted on luck. Instead he expected order, the *natural* sequence of behavior, the cause producing the *natural* effect, the human behaving in a way it was *natural* to behave. He counted on that and upon his own ability to sort out the chaos of observed facts and find in them this *natural* order. It was a talent which caused him, when the facts refused to fall into the pattern demanded by *nature* and the Navajo Way, acute mental discomfort.[27] [Emphasis added]

It is this faith in "the Navajo Way" that motivates Leaphorn to pursue a case. "Somewhere in this jumble of contradictions, oddities, coincidences and unlikely events there must be a pattern, a reason, something that linked cause and effect, which the laws of natural harmony and reason would dictate. It had to be there."[28]

But Navajo culture helps in more specific ways as well. As an apprentice Navajo singer, Jim Chee is training to perform in ceremonies designed to restore the harmony of existence when it has been disturbed by "witches" or "skinwalkers." These are individuals who turn into dangerous animals by night but look normal during the day. Although Chee doesn't literally believe in witches, his understanding encompasses the symbolic truth of "evil beneath a benign mask," a concept central to the unraveling of a case in any detective novel.

In the same way Leaphorn can turn to the Navajo emergence myth to understand greed, the universal basis for evil in the detective novel, as the same kind of witchery. "When the water rose in the Fourth World and the Holy People emerged through a hollow reed, First Man and First Woman came up too. But they forgot witchcraft and they sent Diving Heron back for it. They told him to bring out 'the ways to get rich.' "[29] Witchery, a form of criminal deception, and greed have the same origin. With this kind of insight and motivation it is not surprising that Jim Chee and Joe Leaphorn solve the cases that baffle their Anglo counterparts despite all their sophisticated equipment.

It would no doubt be easy to demonstrate that neither Hillerman nor Berger gives his readers an accurate account of Native American life and culture. The archaeological record suggests that pre-Columbian tribes suffered ecological disasters, and a tourist stopped for speeding by the Navajo tribal police should not expect to be told to "walk in beauty." Like their predecessors, both of these contemporary authors turn to the West and its mythical traditions for an analogy for the present. The persuasiveness of their vision does not depend on their historical accuracy but on its consistency. It draws upon general Western literary conventions as well as the distinctive cultural values that American culture has come to attribute to the Southwest.

It appears that we can communicate insights into the present only by expressing them in comparisons to images and motifs from the past. As the New World has always been somewhere in the West, artists who want to explore the idea of America have almost inevitably turned to western images and motifs. The result is that compared to the sheer quantity of fiction and fine art relating to the West, all other areas and periods in American history appear neglected, even such historically crucial times as the American Revolution or the Civil War. This is true not only in American literature and art but in foreign cultures as well; everywhere the Marlborough Man is the emblem for America. The myth of the American West has found appeal around the world for it is the myth of possibility, the possibility of escape to a place free from the limitations of the present. Of all the possible locales in the West, the Southwest has been the most distinctive for the expression of this myth in literature, art, and popular fiction. Essentially, the mythical West means the Southwest.

Visions of the Southwest have varied by time and place as different audiences project their own dreams onto it. It may be the place for unspoiled wilderness or the place for unfettered economic growth; but as everybody's second homeland, everybody's dream home, the Southwest and America have a difficult role to fulfill, for great expectations inevitably lead to great frustrations. It is a tension that has dominated the image of America and the Southwest and is likely to continue to do so as long as the West remains the dreamland of the world.

NOTES

1. Charles Sealsfield, *Sämtliche Werke*, 25 vols. (Hildesheim, New York: Olms, 1972), vol. 3, p. 215. All translations from Sealsfield's German are my own.
2. Ibid., pp. 21–22.
3. Charles Seatsfield [*sic*], *Life in the New World; or, Sketches of American Society* (New York: J. Winchester, 1844).
4. Charles Sealsfield, *Das Kajütenbuch*, ed. A. Ritter (Stuttgart: Reclam, 1982), pp. 17–18.
5. Ibid., p. 120.

6. Ibid., pp. 20–21.

7. Friedrich Gerstäcker, *Gesammelte Schriften*, 43 vols. (Jena Costenoble, 1872–79), vol. 8, p. 190. All translations from Gerstäcker's German are my own.

8. Ibid., vol. 6, p. 83.

9. Ibid., vol. 4, p. 186.

10. Ibid., vol. 6, p. 167.

11. Quoted in Andrew J. Consentino, *The Paintings of Charles Bird King* (Washington, D.C.: Smithsonian Institution Press for National Collection of Fine Arts, 1977), p. 66.

12. Quoted in Brian W. Dippie, *Remington and Russell* (Austin: University of Texas Press, 1982), p. 11.

13. Zane Grey, *Desert Gold* (1913; reprint, New York: Simon and Schuster, 1969), p. 70.

14. Ibid., p. 277.

15. Owen Wister, *The Virginian* (New York: MacMillan Co., 1960), p. 120.

16. Ibid., pp. 122–23.

17. Ibid., p. 125.

18. Ibid., p. x.

19. Ibid., p. viii.

20. Quoted in Peggy Samuels and Harold Samuels, *Frederic Remington: A Biography* (Garden City, N.Y.: Doubleday, 1982), p. 177.

21. Thomas Berger, *Little Big Man* (New York: Delacorte, 1964), p. 370.

22. Ibid., p. 100.

23. Ibid., p. 253.

24. Ibid., pp. 227–28.

25. Ibid., p. 441.

26. Ibid., p. 444.

27. Tony Hillerman, *The Blessing Way* (New York: Harper and Row, 1970), p. 177.

28. Tony Hillerman, *Listening Woman* (New York: Harper and Row, 1978), p. 30.

29. Hillerman, *The Blessing Way*, p. 88.